© 2017 by Exodus Cry. All rights reserved.

Contributors: Helen Taylor, Blaire Fraim, Tim Fraim, Rebecca Bender, Kezia Hatfield, Courtney Means.

Book design and layout by Kyle Kettler, www.kylekettler.com
Edited by Edited by Lindy Lowry, Kathleen Shryock and Annika Bergen.
Cover photography: Helen Taylor

Special thanks to Rebecca Bender, for providing a survivor-informed perspective on the manual. Visit her website for more information and resources: www.rebeccabender.org

Unless otherwise specified, all Scripture quotations are taken from the Holy Bible, New International Version®, NIV®. Copyright © 1973, 1978, 1984, 2011 by Biblica, Inc.™ Used by permission of Zondervan. All rights reserved worldwide. www.zondervan.com. The "NIV" and "New International Version" are trademarks registered in the United States Patent and Trademark Office by Biblica, Inc.™
Scripture quotations marked (NKJV) are taken from the New King James Version®. Copyright © 1982 by Thomas Nelson. Used by permission. All rights reserved.

Scripture quotations marked ERV are taken from the Easy-to-Read Version (ERV). Copyright © 2006 World Bible Translation Center. The Easy-to-Read Version (ERV) is an English translation of the Bible by the World Bible Translation Center (WBTC), a subsidiary of Bible League International. Used by permission. All rights reserved.
All names were changed to protect the identities of the exploited individuals.

No part of this book may be reproduced, stored in a retrieval system, or transmitted in any form or by any means—electronic, mechanical, photocopy, recording, or, otherwise—without prior written permission of the publisher, except for brief quotations used in connection with reviews in magazines or newspapers.

Ordering information:
Contact intervention@exoduscry.com or visit store at www.exoduscry.com

ISBN: 978-0-9979949-1-9

Second Edition
Printed in the United States

We hope that the information contained in this manual is helpful in your efforts to reach those trapped in commercial sexual exploitation! We also want to let you know that outreach of the nature described in this manual ("Intervention Outreach") is inherently dangerous, even when conducted using the utmost care and caution. By reading this manual and implementing any portion of the recommendations contained herein, YOU EXPRESSLY ACKNOWLEDGE THAT THERE ARE CERTAIN INHERENT RISKS AND DANGERS ASSOCIATED WITH YOUR PARTICIPATION IN INTERVENTION OUTREACH, including, but not limited to, physical injury and/or death. These injuries or outcomes may arise from your own or other's actions, inactions, or negligence, or the condition of the Intervention Outreach's location or facility(ies). Nonetheless, you assume all risks of your participation in Intervention Outreach, whether known or unknown to you.

Further, you hereby expressly RELEASE, WAIVE, DISCHARGE AND COVENANT NOT TO SUE the author, contributors, and Exodus Cry, Inc., including its officers, directors, employees, agents, affiliates, successors and assigns from and for any liability resulting from any personal injury, accident or illness (including death), and/or property loss, however caused, arising from, or in any way related to, your participation in Intervention Outreach, except for those caused by the willful misconduct, gross negligence or intentional torts of the above parties, as applicable.

If you do not agree to any of the statements contained above, you agree to return this manual to Exodus Cry, Inc., for a full refund of the amount you paid for the manual plus reasonable costs for shipping the manual back to Exodus Cry, and to implement no portion of the recommendations and information contained in this manual.

EXODUS CRY

Intervention Manual:
A Guide for Reaching Those Caught in the Sex Industry

Contents

SECTION 1

Intervention 101

10

A Day in the Life: Vulnerable: Vanessa's Story (part 1)	**12**
Trafficking: The Facts	**15**
Eye-Opening Stats	**20**
Redefining "Rescue"	**22**
The Heart and Mind of an Outreach Worker	**25**
Rock Bottom to Real Freedom: Missy's Story	**30**

Contributors:

Blaire Fraim
Helen Taylor

SECTION 2

Online Intervention

32

A Day in the Life: Trafficked: Vanessa's Story (part 2)	**34**
Online Exploitation: The Facts	**36**
Online Outreach	**44**
Building Relationships	**54**
Death to Life: Ruby's Story	**60**
In Her Shoes Project	**63**

Contributors:

Helen Taylor

SECTION 3

Street, Strip Club and Jail Outreach

68

A Day in the Life: Pimped: Vanessa's Story (part 3)	**70**
Pimp Tactics 101	**72**
Street Outreach	**75**
Strip Club Outreach	**84**
Outreach to Jails	**87**
A Brief Encounter: Monica's Story	**90**

Contributors:

Helen Taylor
Blaire Fraim

SECTION 4
Intervention in Community

94

A Day in the Life: Rescued: Vanessa's Story (part 4)	**96**
Building Sustainable Inreach and Outreach Communities	**98**
Being Prepared: Researching an Exit Plan	**103**
Imperative Security Measures	**106**
Sexual Integrity	**111**
Men in Outreach	**116**
Breakthrough by Prayer: Gabriella's Story	**121**

Contributors:
Blaire Fraim
Helen Taylor
Tim Fraim

SECTION 5
Resources

124

Working with Law Enforcement	**126**
Trauma and Self-Care	**128**
Recommended Reading	**140**
The Current Landscape of Exploitation	**146**
Legal Approaches to Prostitution Legalization Worldwide	**152**

Contributors:
Helen Taylor
Kezia Hatfield

SECTION 6
Endnotes and Appendix

162

Endnotes	**164**
Appendix A: Texting Scripts	**169**
Appendix B: Setting Up Google Voice	**179**
Appendix C: Sexual Integrity Commitment Form	**180**
Appendix D: Confidentiality Form	**181**
Appendix E: Reporting Forms	**185**
Appendix F: Meeting Form	**186**
Appendix G: History Form	**188**
Appendix H: Palermo Protocols	**191**

Prologue

When I was 16 years old, I remember somehow getting lost in my home city of London, U.K., and finding myself in the red-light district in Soho. Neon-lit sex shops, peep shows, and strip clubs lined the narrow alleyways and my pulse quickened as I tried to find my way out. Walking briskly down the alley, I saw a young woman standing in a doorway leaning against the bricks. She looked Eastern European. Her hair was dyed blonde and she was wearing a red silk dress. Her face was resigned and there was a hauntingly sad expression in her eyes.

As I left the area and traveled home on the train, I was struck with two distinct emotions: 1) the horrifying reality of prostitution—that any random man could walk up and pay to rent this young woman's body for sex for a few dehumanizing minutes, and 2) an overwhelming sense of God's love and compassion for her.

For several minutes on the train, my heart beat furiously as I contemplated returning and giving her a rose (but at age 16 I was too embarrassed to do so, in case it might offend her). I just wanted to give her some tangible token of her worth and beauty, for her to realize that her purpose as a woman was far beyond being a deposit for a man's momentary violent pleasure.

It wasn't until a few years later that I learned more about sex trafficking and the modern-day pandemic of this form of slavery and exploitation. But the vivid memory of the young woman in the red dress has always stayed with me.

The city of London saw two great abolitionists rise up during the 18th and 19th centuries: William Wilberforce (who famously abolished the transatlantic slave trade) and then William Booth (who founded the Salvation Army, which largely focused on helping the poor and destitute—including those in prostitution). These two heroes of the faith witnessed huge shifts in cultural mindsets. They saw laws changed and the church mobilized towards social justice in unprecedented ways. Interestingly, this all took place during the nationwide Methodist revival. In the Kingdom of God, revival and justice are often intertwined.

In the last few years, there has been a notable spotlight on the issue of slavery once again, and sex trafficking has been exposed as one of the greatest modern-day evils of our time. Most of society is in agreement that slavery is wrong. However, I pray my generation witnesses a paramount shift in our cultural mindset—to recognize prostitution to be the world's oldest oppression, not "profession," and an inherent form of violence against women and children.

In Luke 10, Jesus tells the well-known parable of the Good Samaritan. It is ultimately Christ's love that compels us to open our eyes and see the violated, bloody, naked individual. Instead of turning away and walking by, will we be those who would leave our comfort zones and intervene, offering compassion and assistance? Jesus shares this scenario to show us the highest expression of loving our neighbor. In addition, we find Jesus Himself in the face of the poor, the needy, the prisoner, and the oppressed (Matthew 25). When we love them, we are truly loving Him.

God is seeking friends and advocates who will take a stand and bear witness to the God of the Bible who longs to bring justice to the vulnerable and oppressed, the widows and orphans of our culture. We, the body of Christ, are called to act as Jesus' hands and feet; and to embody His compassion and empathy; to visit them in their trouble and demonstrate His Kingdom and love in a fully active partnership. The church, His partner and Bride, is surely the Lord's Plan A to bring justice to the world!

In this survivor-informed manual, we outline what we believe to be the strategies and best practices to reach those in the sex industry, whether it be on the streets, in strip clubs, in jails, or through online venues. A large portion of this manual focuses on outreach to those sold for sex over the internet, since much of prostitution has moved online and the internet has swiftly become the world's largest brothel.

Our prayer is that this manual will be an inspiring and effective resource to help you gain a deeper understanding of this injustice, equip you to reach those caught in the nightmare of trafficking and commercial sexual exploitation, and teach you how to carry your heart in the midst of the journey.

We pray that you'll benefit from our experiences and testimonies and feel empowered to join a growing army of modern-day abolitionists that God is raising up from the grassroots level to the highest governmental offices. Compelled by Christ's relentless love, this army is committed to advocate for the ending of the injustice of human trafficking. For those of us called to frontline outreach, we are committed to going into the darkest places, so that His blazing light would shine brightly and His love would be made known. It is our hope and honor to then empower and walk alongside the individuals we meet on their journey from darkness into light. We want to see God transform shame into redemption and unfathomable abuse into their calling and true destiny.

Consider the glorious mission of our Ultimate Abolitionist Jesus Christ, who publicly announced in Luke 4 that He came to preach Good News to the poor, to heal the brokenhearted, to proclaim liberty to the captives and recovery of sight to the blind, and to set at liberty those who are oppressed.

How wonderful that He invites you and me to join Him in bringing the gospel of His Good News to those without hope. What could our trembling response to this beautiful invitation be but to simply say: "Here am I Lord...send me"?

Helen Taylor
Director of Intervention
Exodus Cry

SECTION 1:
Intervention 101

12

A Day in the Life: Vulnerable: Vanessa's Story (part 1)

PART 1
15

Trafficking: The Facts
Eye-Opening Stats

PART 2
22

Redefining "Rescue"

PART 3
25

The Heart and Mind of an Outreach Worker

30

Rock Bottom to Real Freedom: Missy's Story

A DAY IN THE LIFE
Vulnerable: Vanessa's Story

In abolition work, minimizing factors that make people vulnerable to being trafficked is key to prevention. Listen in to Vanessa's story, told in her own words. Vanessa's journey of instability highlights several common preludes to a young girl succumbing to the lures of a recruiter or pimp.

Vanessa's story:

I experienced an unconventional childhood. My parents' drug and alcohol addictions meant they were frequently uprooting and moving whenever a drug deal went south. I grew up everywhere, which had a negative impact on my education. At age 18, I could barely read. Socially, forming deep friendships was difficult. We always had to make new friends at new schools. I didn't even want to make new friends 'cause I knew we were going to move anyway. I didn't have any say in these moves, and that impacted my sense of free will. Even when I was little, I never had a choice of what I wanted. I was taught that saying "no" was never an option; I was to do what I was told.

When I was just six years old, my father got into a fight with a drug dealer. He didn't have the money to pay him, and the dealer lashed out in anger. The dealer masked himself and broke into our house. He violently smothered to death my baby sister in her bed. The dealer ran away, but my father found him and killed him, and was later arrested and sent to prison.

I mourned the absence of my father. However, after his release, he returned to the family a more angry and violent man. He was verbally and physically abusive toward me in particular. He always took it out on me when he was mad. One day, I went to school with black eyes and marks on my body, so the school called child protective services and told them I was being beaten. At age 12, I was placed in foster care, which sadly was another traumatizing life event for me, especially because none my other siblings were removed with me (I was the middle child). Over the next few years, I lived in four different foster homes and suffered sexual abuse from a foster father and another boy in one of the homes. My sense of ownership over my body was torn away from me, and being passed from home to home made me feel unwanted and unloved.

> *"Trafficking is simply an exploitation of vulnerability."*
>
> —Lauran Bethell, human trafficking consultant and interviewee in *Nefarious: Merchant of Souls*[1]

Intervention Manual

By the time I was 18, I was ready to leave foster care and get on my feet. I was a single mom with a young daughter and was determined to find a job. While I looked for work, I was sent to a women's shelter. Because my reading skills were poor, finding a job proved difficult. After three months, I was desperate. Right about that time, I received a text from an old high school friend asking how I was doing and where I was staying. I told her the name of the shelter and that I was still looking for work. What I didn't know was that this high school friend had been trafficked and was being used to recruit me by finding out about my situation and whereabouts. The very next day, the trafficker began circling the shelter in his truck, observing my daughter and me from afar. After three days, he approached me saying, "I've got a job if you want to apply for it." He told me it was an office job. When I admitted I'd never worked in an office and couldn't read properly, he said, "That's okay. I'm looking for someone I can train and teach things to." It seemed I was in the right place at the right time. Here was the opportunity I'd been hoping for! I collected my things and got in his truck.

The trafficker, Rocco, did not have an office job for Vanessa, and his version of "training her" would look very different than what she expected. He strategically chose her, using her friend to obtain key information about Vanessa, not only about her location and situation, but also about her character and background. In America, exploited girls frequently report a rocky history in foster care and a lack of support from a stable family unit or protective community. Past sexual abuse also can be a strong coercive force that greatly heightens a girl's vulnerability and the likelihood she'll be preyed upon.

Vanessa's story demonstrates additional key factors that serve to make a girl more vulnerable to recruiting tactics.

Common vulnerabilities traffickers prey upon:
- Educational instability and illiteracy
- Financial pressure to provide for herself (and a dependent child)
- Lack of practical job skills
- Poverty
- Single parent
- Lack of family support
- Physical abuse
- Sexual abuse
- Low self-esteem

PART 1:
Trafficking: The Facts

Before we can start to intervene and push back the darkness that overshadows millions of victims, we need to first identify some of the basic terms and definitions that characterize human trafficking.

What Is Trafficking?

The U.S. Department of Health and Human Services defines trafficking in persons two ways:

Definition 1	Definition 2
Sex trafficking in which a commercial sex act is induced by force, fraud, or coercion, or in which the person induced to perform such act has not attained 18 years of age. If a victim is younger than 18, force, fraud, or coercion is not necessary to prove trafficking. A minor being sold for sex is automatically considered a victim of trafficking.	The recruitment, harboring, transportation, provision, or obtaining of a person for labor or services through the use of force, fraud, or coercion for the purpose of subjection to involuntary servitude, peonage, debt bondage, or slavery. It is a crime against humanity.

Who Is Particularly Vulnerable to Commercial Sexual Exploitation?

- **Runaways:** According to the National Center for Missing and Exploited Children, as many as 2.8 million children in the United States run away from home each year. Within 48 hours of hitting the streets, one-third of these children are lured or recruited into the underground world of prostitution and pornography.

- **Childhood sexual abuse:** Estimates of the prevalence of incest among prostituted persons range from 65 percent to 90 percent.[2]

- **Foster care:** Most girls in the United States who end up in prostitution have been through the foster care system at some point in their childhoods. In 2013, 60 percent of the child sex trafficking victims recovered as part of an FBI nationwide raid from over 70 cities were children from foster care or group homes.[33]

- **Desperate for love:** In her book, *The Prostitution of Sexuality*, Kathleen Barry, co-founder of the Coalition Against Trafficking in Women, writes: *"Pimps target girls or women who seem naïve, lonely, homeless, and rebellious. At first, the attention and feigned affection from the pimp convinces her to 'be his woman.' Pimps ultimately keep prostituted women in virtual captivity by verbal abuse—making a woman feel that she is utterly worthless; and by physical coercion, beatings and the threat of torture. 80 to 95 percent of all prostitution is pimp-controlled."*[4]

- **Race:** Black, Hispanic, and indigenous women are disproportionally vulnerable and targeted for prostitution. *"Women in prostitution are purchased for their appearance, including skin color and characteristics based on ethnic stereotyping. Throughout history, women have been enslaved and prostituted based on race and ethnicity, as well as gender"* (Vednita Carter, Melissa Farley).[5]

Prostitution vs. Sex Trafficking

If any individual has entered the sex industry under force, fraud, or coercion, they are a trafficking victim. Although not every person in prostitution or the pornography industry legally falls into this category, many do. All minors (under age 18) in the sex industry are automatically classified as trafficking victims, irrelevant of consent.

Unfortunately, by categorizing individuals into distinct boxes of "trafficked" or "prostitute," we can end up classifying victims as "worthy" or "unworthy."

Prostitution survivor Rachel Moran explains:

"By drawing distinctions between trafficking and prostitution, between under and over eighteen, some well-intentioned anti-trafficking organizations acquiesce to the perpetuation of a system known to be extremely violent and damaging while continuing to

stigmatize and blame most of its victims. This stigmatization maintains the disempowerment and marginalization of the same population these groups want to help. It also empowers the predators who prey on our most vulnerable, whether under or over eighteen.

Choice does not always present as balanced; it does not always offer a different-but-equal alternative. When I think of my choices there were simply these: have men on and inside you, or continue to suffer homelessness and hunger. Take your pick. Make your 'choice'."[6]

Recognizing the concept of "choice" to be extremely complex, we believe it is important to focus less on qualifying the circumstances that led an individual into prostitution or the pornography set, and instead to emphasize the violence and trauma induced within the system of the sex industry.

Prostitution could be comparable to an individual ravaged by a beast within a Roman gladiatorial arena. Whether she entered by being dragged inside by a third party, was given false information about what the path led to, or out of curiosity was drawn into the arena by the lights and noise of the crowd, the point is that she is currently in an arena with a beast and needs help. Her precise path for getting there should be the secondary issue.

The activist Dorchen A. Leidholdt argues: *"Prostitution and sex trafficking are the same human rights catastrophe ... Both are part of a system of gender-based domination that makes violence against women and girls profitable to a mind-boggling extreme. Both prey on women and girls made vulnerable by poverty, discrimination, and violence and leave them traumatized, sick, and impoverished. The concerted effort by some NGO's and governments to disconnect trafficking from prostitution—to treat them as distinct and unrelated phenomena—is nothing less than a deliberate political strategy aimed at legitimizing the sex industry and protecting its growth and profitability."*[7]

Forms of Commercial Sex Industry Exploitation

The commercial sex industry refers to any venue or system that makes a profit from the sexual exploitation of a man, woman, or child—such as prostitution, pornography, stripping, or massage parlors, to name a few. Wherever sex is for sale, trafficking will follow. For example, while not every person in a strip club is being trafficked, you will often find individuals who are being prostituted, coerced, or controlled. Below, we take a closer look at the various forms of commercial sexual exploitation:

 Strip clubs: Throughout all 50 states in America, strip clubs harbor victims of both sex and labor trafficking who may be forced or coerced into providing commercial sex to club patrons by a pimp, employer, or outside controller. Most strippers report being propositioned for sex by the men who frequent the clubs where they work. Stripping is often a gateway into prostitution.

 Pornography: Many times porn performers have a history of abuse, poverty, and drug addiction. Like prostitution, a third party pays them to perform sex acts. The only difference between prostitution and performing in a porn film is the presence of a camera, which makes it legal. In many situations, the agent or producer is simply a glorified pimp.

 Online prostitution: In the United States, the internet is the primary venue through which traffickers, pimps, and johns buy and sell sex from women and children. Many victims are forced to post and monitor their own ads on classified advertising sites. They may appear to be working on their own, but in reality, girls are usually threatened with violence and other forms of abuse by their exploiter if they do not meet a certain financial goal each night.

 Street prostitution: You may find it surprising to learn that 89 percent of U.S. women currently involved in prostitution say they want out but believe they have no other options. Without this information, people may find it easy to judge a stranger and assume she chose this life and therefore isn't worth reaching out to. The truth is that most people caught in sexual exploitation feel as if they have no other choice, and their perceptions of having no choices perpetuates their exploitation.

> Although all forms of prostitution are inherently violent and dangerous in nature, street prostitution has unique risks. Exploited victims have little ability to control their environment and are at the mercy of the men who pick them up The pro-prostitution lobbyists have leveraged the violence against prostituted women on the streets as a rationale to regulate indoor prostitution and to provide clean and safe working environments for them. This mindset only legitimizes sex work and sets a context for state-sponsored pimping. Prostitution and the sale of sexual services are inherent forms of violence committed against men, women, and children, and we believe that the purchase of sex should not be tolerated or legalized under any circumstance.

Escort services: Escort services are another common front for sex trafficking. Victims may be forced to provide commercial sex, including "out-call" services (the individual goes to the john's location) or "in-call" services (the john comes to the individual's location). These appointments are generally controlled and arranged by an agency, pimp, or other controller who may keep an eye on the exploited person through a third party. Escort services are commonly advertised online through specific escort websites as well as public websites.

Truck stops: Sex trafficking occurs at truck stops in multiple ways but most commonly through pimp-controlled prostitution. Pimps frequently move their victims from city to city, forcing them to engage in commercial sex at truck stops along the route.

Sugar daddies: Sugar daddies are wealthy, older men who give money or gifts to younger females (or males), termed "sugar babies," in return for sexual favors (and companionship). This has become a recent phenomenon, with several websites set up to arrange such "partnerships." Youth in financial hardships or college debt are often vulnerable targets.

Brothels: Anywhere prostitution takes place that involves more than one exploited individual qualifies as a brothel. However, brothels are often disguised as massage parlors, strip clubs, or studios. Women typically live on site where they are often confined and coerced into providing commercial sex. In the United States, these locations are often fronted by an Asian massage parlor claiming to offer legitimate services.

Eye-Opening Stats

"Reliable statistics related to human trafficking are difficult to find. Human trafficking is a clandestine crime, and few victims and survivors come forward for fear of retaliation, shame, or lack of understanding of what is happening to them. Numbers are not always the story. Pursue individual stories of survival, new government initiatives, or innovative research efforts until better data are available" (U.S. State Department Trafficking in Persons Report, 2014).

An estimated

40-42 MILLION

people are in prostitution globally.

An estimated

99%

of sex buyers are men.

99%

of sex trafficking victims are women.

70%

of female trafficking victims are trafficked into the commercial sex industry (this includes porn, strip clubs, and massage parlors in the US).

Human trafficking is the fastest growing criminal industry. Sex trafficking generates

$99 BILLION-PLUS

per year.

Intervention Manual

Global

- An estimated 40-42 million people are in prostitution globally (Fondation Scelles Report, 2012).

- Out of that number, an estimated 75 percent of victims are between 13-25 years old (Fondation Scelles Report, 2012).

- Whereas 99.9 percent of sex buyers are men whereas 99 percent of sex trafficking victims are women (or identify as women) (International Labor Organization, 2016). However, we know that boys who are victims of sex trafficking are underreported worldwide, so that figure is likely higher than 1 percent.

- After drug trafficking, human trafficking ties with the illegal arms industry as the second-largest criminal industry in the world today. It is the fastest-growing criminal industry, sex trafficking generates an estimated $99 per year (International Labor Organization, 2014).

- According to 18 estimates from 10 countries, most people in prostitution are pimped or trafficked (84 peercent, ranging from 50 percent to 99 percent Farley et al. 3619 with 14 of the 18 estimates falling between 80 percent and 90 percent; Farley, Franzblau, & Kennedy, 2014).

- Most sex trafficking is regional or national and is perpetrated by traffickers who are the same nationality as their victims (United Nations, Global Report on Trafficking in Persons, 2009).

- Countries that are the highest culprits for sourcing trafficking victims include Albania, Belarus, Bulgaria, China, Lithuania, Nigeria, Moldova, Romania, Russia, Thailand, and Ukraine (UNODC's 2012 Trafficking in Persons: Global Patterns).

- Countries that are the highest culprits for being the final destination of trafficked victims are Belgium, Germany, Greece, Israel, Italy, Japan, Netherlands, Thailand, Turkey, and the USA (UNODC's 2012 Trafficking in Persons: Global Patterns).

- In one study, 89 percent of 854 people in prostitution from nine countries said that they wanted to escape prostitution, but 75 percent needed a home or safe place, 76 percent needed job training, 61 percent needed health care, 56 percent needed individual counseling, 51 percent needed peer support, 51 percent needed legal assistance, and 47 percent needed drug/alcohol treatment (M. Farley, Prostitution Research, 2003).

United States

- While there is no official estimate of the total number of human trafficking victims in the United States, Polaris Project (an organization working to combat human trafficking) estimates that the total number of victims nationally reaches into the hundreds of thousands when estimates of both adults and minors and sex trafficking and labor trafficking are aggregated (Polaris Project, 2012).

- One in five runaways reported to the National Center for Missing and Exploited Children in 2015 were likely victims of sex trafficking—up from one in seven in 2013. Of these likely sex trafficking victims, 74 percent were in the care of social services or foster care when they ran away (The National Center for Missing and Exploited Children).

- A 2014 report estimated that the underground sex economy ranged from $39.9 million in Denver, Colorado, to $290 million in Atlanta, Georgia (The Urban Institute, 2014).

- Approximately 75-83 percent of documented sex trafficked victims between 2008 and 2010 were United States citizens.[8]

- The Polaris Project conservatively estimates that a pimp with a "stable" of three girls or women often enforces an average nightly quota of $500, or $1,500 a night. If these quotas are met consistently, the pimp can make as much as $547,000 (or more) in a year ($1,500 a night x 365 nights a year = $547,500). (The Polaris Project, "Street Prostitution," 2010).

- Seventy percent of females who are victims of human trafficking are trafficked into the commercial sex industry (This includes porn, strip clubs, and massage parlors in the U.S.) (U.S. Department of Justice, 2004).

Intervention 101

PART 2:
Redefining "Rescue"

Often, we have a romanticized idea of rescue shaped more by Hollywood than by reality. A critical part of intervention involves having an accurate understanding of trafficking and the coercive elements present—leading to the victim's complicity in her own exploitation. Thus, rescue is rarely a grab-and-go event; it is a journey.

The statistics show us that hundreds of thousands of adult and minor-age (under 18) trafficking victims are being forced to prostitute themselves in underground networks. These victims, especially minors, need an intervention. However, as we noted earlier, many adult men and women involved in the commercial sex industry initially were forced into prostitution as minors or under circumstances that would classify them as having been trafficked. These adults do not always require a "physical rescue"; the "chains" that keep them in commercial sexual exploitation are psychological and emotional, not as obvious to an outsider but just as real.

Rarely do exploited individuals identify themselves as "victims." They have been forced to survive, and survival makes people do things they would never normally agree to—due to brainwashing, trauma, trauma-bonding, and lack of other opportunities or choices.

"Rescue" Is a Process, Not Just a One-Time Event

Often, fear of the unknown is greater than fear of facing continued exploitation each day. Facing the obstacles that come as exploited individuals seek freedom takes great courage and determination. Think about the newly freed children of Israel who often wanted to return to Egypt when they faced obstacles.

Christ loves us freely, perfectly, completely, and with no agenda. He lays His heart bare before us and has given us free will to choose to accept that love or reject it. Freedom isn't free; it costs us everything. Jesus showed us that the cost of freedom is surrender.

We meet exploited individuals in the places of their greatest pain, shame, and desperation. In that place, we have the opportunity to share with them glimpses of the true freedom that comes from living for a greater purpose. Our hearts must be focused on building bridges into a person's isolation and shame, and then walking alongside them as they cross over from death into life.

> *"There is no pit so deep that God's love is not deeper still."*
> **–Corrie ten Boom**

Ultimately, that decision is theirs and theirs alone.

For many, the opportunities to have a childhood, a family, and a voice were stolen at a young age. The choice they make now to walk out of exploitation and into the light is the first step they will take toward rebuilding their own free will. Understanding the dignity of our free will is a gateway to experiencing the beauty of the love of Christ. In her memoir, *The Hiding Place*, Holocaust survivor Corrie ten Boom writes, "There is no pit so deep that God's love is not deeper still."

Moved by Compassion

Part of redefining rescue is understanding the true sacrifice and impact of compassion. While most people understand the word "compassion" to mean feelings of empathy or care, based on the Latin roots of the word, it means, "to suffer with." The Bible defines compassion in several ways: We are to "speak up for those who cannot speak for themselves and defend the rights of the poor and needy" (Prov. 31: 8-9). Think about the example of the Good Samaritan (Luke 10), who risks his life and makes a great sacrifice to come to the aid of the man left for dead. He was moved with compassion.

"Compassion is hard because it requires the inner disposition to go with others to the place where they are weak, vulnerable, lonely, and broken." —author Henri Nouwen, *Compassion: A Reflection on the Christian Life*

The true meaning of compassion requires us to open our hearts and compels us to ask hard but necessary questions:

- **Are we willing to pay the cost with our actions (not just our words) to show true compassion to see exploited victims freed?**

- **Are we willing to invest our time, money, safety, and reputations to have compassion on those who have been left for dead?**

- **Are we willing to look beyond their situation and see greatness inside of them?**

Jesus declared His earthly mandate in Luke's gospel:

> "The Spirit of the Lord is upon me, because he has anointed me to proclaim good news to the poor. He has sent me to proclaim freedom for the prisoners and recovery of sight for the blind, to set the oppressed free."
>
> Luke 4:18

Our message must transcend their bondage. Everything the world has to offer leaves these men and women thirsting for more; tortured in the accusations of the enemy and trapped in self-pity and entitlement. We must speak something eternal into the natural—burning with the truth about freedom. Just as Jesus announced His mission (to free the oppressed), we have been called to that same purpose: to see the captives set free and walking in their true identities as children of God. We must go to them, rebuke the oppressor, and journey with them towards healing and everlasting life.

"Our message must transcend their bondage."

PART 3:
The Heart and Mind of an Outreach Worker

At Exodus Cry, we assist individuals who are currently being trafficked or exploited through the commercial sex industry.

Our passion for and advocacy for victims of trafficking doesn't end when they turn 18 or when a camera is placed in the room and a girl becomes a "porn star" rather than a prostituted woman. We must look beyond labels and definitions and into the hearts for all those we are fighting to see freed and restored.

Our Shared, Sustaining Values

To unify our team in our mission, we embrace and practice shared values that work together—foundational values that support, guide, and sustain us on our journey. Below, we have listed our shared values and how they describe the heart and mind of an outreach worker.

> *"Love with no agenda."*

First and foremost, the truth, simplicity, power, and eternal reality of the love of Christ provide our motivation, plumb line, and solution: We love because God first loved us. Our love for those we minister to can only be authentic and sustained if this compassionate love is an overflow or outworking of our love for Him. As the apostle Paul wrote in his letter to Corinth, if we don't have love, we have nothing: "Though I speak with the tongues of men and of angels, but have not love, I have become sounding brass or a clanging cymbal" (1 Cor. 13:1).

> **Love in the name of Jesus: Our love is not passive; it is active and living. It compels us. This love is rooted in our identity as the sons and daughters of God. We don't need to hide that fact, but we also don't have to preach it or force it upon someone. Our goal for outreach cannot be "successful evangelism" or even Christian conversion. Our goal must be to love and build a relationship established in trust.**

Love with no agenda: This is the hardest value to maintain during this kind of outreach. As Christians, we have good intentions, and we want the best for the women and children we seek to serve. But we must understand that even our best intentions can often cause harm.

If we want anything (including what we would perceive as good things) from an exploited person, we become just like many others in their lives who use them, take from them, or impress their wills upon them. The laying down of our agendas, our good intentions, and our expectations is critical to loving exploited persons well and in a way that empowers them to make their own choices rather than pressuring them to do what we want them to do.

Agendas are subtle and coated in the best intentions. We want to see people free, out of prostitution. We want them to know Christ. We want them to make good choices for their betterment. But our love and our support should never come with strings attached. Jesus' life and death are our best model for loving with no agenda. His love for us is not based on our performance, our ability to do good things, or our results. His love is freely given. It is perfect, and unchanging in its fervency. He desires our good in all things, but our choice to heed His voice and apply His wisdom does not impact His love for us or His acceptance. What a beautiful mystery—His invitation to us is to love like He loves. We can only practice this kind of love if we remain in Him.

Love that Goes the Distance

As we enter into relationships with exploited victims, we often get a front-row seat to witness Jesus' transformation in their lives. However, this kind of change rarely happens immediately. The journey is littered with destructive choices, pain, and heartbreak. But as Jesus begins to enter their story, love takes over: Love heals, love restores, love adopts, love transforms. We get to be conduits of His love and faithfulness to His children.

So set your hearts for the long haul. Be willing to invest your time. Be committed, whether that commitment is a one-time meeting or a relationship that lasts for years.

Motivated by Christ, Not the Cause

If our motivation for fighting injustice stems solely from seeing the problem, our hearts will grow weary from the seemingly insurmountable needs. We will become disillusioned when we don't immediately see positive results and cynical from the apathy within our culture. While we must see the need and identify with suffering, our

Intervention Manual

> *"We never graduate from the place of prayer."*

motivation must be rooted in beholding Jesus. When we behold Him, we understand His emotions, His zeal for justice, His commitment to bring about justice, and His ability to do so. An understanding of obedience is key. We are obedient to God's call to fight injustice and free the captives regardless of how or if victims respond.

Isaiah 42 serves as an anchor for us as modern-day abolitionists. In the passage below, God outlines His gospel-centered strategy for justice in partnership with His Church:

"Here is my servant, whom I uphold, my chosen one in whom I delight; I will put my Spirit on him, and he will bring justice to the nations. In faithfulness he will bring forth justice; he will not falter or be discouraged till he establishes justice on earth." (Isa. 42:1-4).

A life of outreach is an overflow of a life of prayer: We never graduate from the place of prayer. Prayer is where we partner with Christ to bring His authority and presence into the darkness we're entering. Prayer is about friendship with God. We don't pray and then go into outreach relying on our own strength to carry and sustain us. Our mission requires that God give us strength. Our prayers for justice are about fellowship with God, and that symbiotic relationship must continue as we enter into justice work.

A community of compassion: As we reach out to exploited people living in isolation, we must have something to offer them. We must be a community that extends compassion to those who have never known community or experienced the unconditional love of a family. In Romans 12:5, Paul tells us that we are an extension of the body of Christ, and we must be able to bring those we're trying to reach into real relationships with that body and then introduce them to the gifts that God has given them:

"So in Christ we, though many, form one body, and each member belongs to all the others. We have different gifts, according to the grace given to each of us" (Rom. 12:5).

Prevailing Against the Darkness

"You are Peter, and on this rock I will build my church and the gates of Hell will not prevail against it" (Matt. 16:8).

Jesus' promise assures us that although we may face great opposition from the enemy, He will overcome. Although it may be easy to look at this verse through a purely spiritual lens, the Lord was also making a powerful statement connected to the physical environment. Jesus made this declaration to Peter in the region of Caesarea Philippi where He strategically brought His disciples. It was the only time in His earthly ministry when He traveled to this northeast region of Israel and the farthest north He went. The region was a renowned center of immorality. Taking the disciples there would have been equivalent to taking them into a red-light district (an area in any city known for prostitution). Yet Jesus had a clear reason for bringing them there.

In the Old Testament this region was known as the center of Baal worship, and in the Roman period, it was where people made child sacrifices to the god Pan. Prostitution occurred, and the most deviant sexual rituals were performed to summon Pan. These pagan worship rituals were centered at the base of Mount Hermon where a large spring—one of the three sources of the Jordan River—formed in the mouth of a cave. To pagans, water symbolized the underworld while caves were believed to be the gates through which spirits traveled from the underworld to ours. The site was literally known as "the gates of Hades."

The disciples would have clearly understood the significance of Jesus' statement in this place. He took them to the most morally corrupt place—the stronghold of false religion, idol worship, and depravity—and laid out a clear message: Here on this rock, My church will be established. Here, where the rocks are carved with false gods, He asked His disciples, "Who do you say I am?" Here, He first revealed that He is the Christ. Here, in this seemingly God-forsaken place, He emphatically declared that there was no place His presence and power cannot transform, and it was here where He commissioned His disciples to build His Church.

> *"He has heard the cries of the afflicted and uses us to send the help they are praying for."*

In the most corrupt, morally bankrupt site in Israel, Jesus commissioned His disciples to confront and challenge the enemy on His ground.

Too often, we've gone on the defensive and shrunk back in fear and intimidation while the enemy has kept the captive bound behind gates of death. But gates are defensive structures. If we are to prevail against the gates of hell as Jesus instructs (and promises), we must be on the offensive, storming those gates.

We storm and break down these gates when we go forth in confidence, remembering that Christ has not only commanded us but has also given us authority to push back the darkness of isolation and to guide victims out of exploitation.

When we enter the life of a sexually exploited individual, we can be confident that the Lord has already gone before us, preparing the way. He has heard the cries of the afflicted and uses us to send the help they are praying for. Several times, we've seen an exploited girl respond to a text message because she believes it could be the answer to a prayer asking God to intervene in her life and provide a way out. This was the case with Missy.

MISSY'S STORY
From Rockbottom to Real Freedom

My teammate and I (Blaire) met Missy at a local community college, where she was taking a course. She was hopeful she could get a medical certification that would allow her to help people. When we offered her a black bag printed with H-O-P-E, she began to realize that we weren't there to recruit her but that we genuinely cared about her. Sometimes the bag, lovingly filled with beauty products and small gifts, can reach a girl's heart faster than our words can. It goes home with her to the place of trouble where we cannot go. It remains with her and declares the truth and the promise of hope. Missy began to open up about her story, her dreams, and her life.

She was from a small midwestern town. At age 12, her dad began to teach her to cook meth. During her teen years, Missy was in and out of foster care, consistently in trouble at school, and suffering from a growing drug addiction. Her chaotic life was a constant fight for survival. At age 18, she was on her own—no longer subjected to the whims of the state. She thought she was finally free to live her own life.

Missy met Troy through a friend. For their first date, he took her to Taco Bell. On the second date, he gave her $10 to spend at Walmart and told her to go buy herself something while he waited in the car. That was all it took for her to call him her boyfriend. She was convinced he truly loved her. He was her pimp; she was his girl. She was 19.

The first time Missy got out of line, Troy gave her a good shiner on her face. Still, she insisted she was special to him, and not like his other girls. He let her keep more of her money than the other girls. She tried to convince herself that he trusted her the most, that she was in charge of the other girls, and that she only worked when she wanted to. Just two months into their relationship, Troy landed in jail for a drug charge. Missy continued in prostitution to support him when he was in jail.

Not long after his conviction, Missy had an encounter with a buyer who pretended to be a cop and threatened her with a Taser. He intimidated her into adhering to his every violent demand. Realizing the reality of her situation and how bad things had become, Missy cried out to God. The next day she received a text from our team who had seen her ad on the "Adult" section of the website Backpage: "Hi!

If you want out of the game, there are people in KC who can help you. Text me if you want to know more." Missy responded. The text was a lifeline in the midst of a storm of exploitation.

We continued to regularly meet with Missy and built a relationship with her, investing in her with our words and our actions. She didn't have enough money for her course textbooks, so we helped her buy them. Her pimp had less control over her from prison, and as she spent more time with us, her weekly visits to him became less frequent. As she began to believe and take in our message that she was a valuable human being, Missy began to understand that she could break the cycle of exploitation and addiction and accomplish her goals.

A couple of weeks after meeting Missy, we took her to a church service. She cried as she heard the gospel, telling us later that she hadn't cried in many years. Her tough-girl persona started to disintegrate before our eyes as she began to share with us memories of childhood trauma, rejection, and violence. Gradually, the truth began to rebuild her as love washed over her and courage filled her with strength.

The final step in Missy's journey toward freedom came four months into our friendship with her. A john held her against her will in a hotel room. For 24 hours, she was held captive, raped, and traumatized. Finally able to escape, she ran to the hotel lobby and called our team for help. She was done. She couldn't do it another day. She wanted to live. She wanted out, fully. Finally.

At that point, we provided a safe place for her to live until we were able to help her transition to a secure support system and get the care she so desperately needed. As a result, Missy was able to get a steady job and began to rebuild her life. We had the honor of walking with her for a brief six-month period. During that time, we provided a safety net and supported her as she took courageous steps to walk away from the devastation of exploitation and into a new life.

SECTION 2:
Online Intervention

34

A Day in the Life: Trafficked: Vanessa's Story (part 2)

PART 1

36

Online Exploitation: The Facts

PART 2

44

Online Outreach

PART 3

54

Building Relationships

60

Death to Life: Ruby's Story

63

In Her Shoes Project

A DAY IN THE LIFE
Trafficked: Vanessa's Story (pt. 2)
[Trigger Warning]

The reality of life within commercial sexual exploitation is horrifying. Told in her own words, Vanessa describes the repeated abuse she survived after her pimp, Rocco, offered her a "job":

My first week was terrifying. On my very first night, Rocco made me see someone. The guy was a regular and was aware that I was new. He still tried having sex with me even though I was crying. He didn't care ... he just wanted to get off. Having sex with random men I didn't know was sickening to me. It made me feel disgusting and helpless. The second man I saw smacked me so hard on my face that my lip piercing flew out. It was ... hard to go through some of that.

> "We had to make a certain kind of money by a certain time, and if we didn't, we'd get into trouble."

The brothel we lived in (which was a large house in a suburban area in the Midwest) was crazy. When I first arrived, there were 18 girls and seven kids. The girls were lost, confused; they didn't know who they were. We all had to work every day. Sometimes we worked from morning 'til night without time to eat or sleep much. We had to stick to a daily beauty regime. We had to make a certain kind of money by a certain time, and if we didn't, we'd get into trouble. There were punishments—Rocco would make us go without sleep for a long period of time. If we fell asleep, he would come into the room and beat us. It was a never-ending process. I felt like I was being used all of the time, just for someone else's needs and wants.

We always had to wear extremely provocative clothing. Even when it was snowing, we had to dress in very little. Rocco made sure that all the girls had makeup and clothes, but not the kind of clothes any of us wanted to wear—just what he thought the girls would make money in.

Rocco would sell us through his friends or as "escorts" online through Backpage.com or a sugar daddy website. This woman named Shelly was the one who made our online profiles. She'd been one of his girls in the past. She made all the calls and set up the appointments. She made sure all the girls got a call.

The calls were usually an hour long, and then you'd go to the next one and then the next one—all kinds of men: Mexican, Chinese, Asian, Black, Army guys, truck drivers. Some were in their 60s. Some were in their 50s or 40s. Some men would want a threesome ... and it was nasty, like really nasty. The client would have sex with both of us girls, and he'd make us do stuff to each other. Most of the men wanted to have sex without protection, but I said, "No." Some would still sneak the condom off. I felt very unsafe. Some girls got pregnant from clients, but they still had to keep working.

We were taken to cities all over the states and even Mexico. The sessions would always be at a hotel or their house. It's a scary situation because you never know what they're going to do to you. They could beat you and rob you, and then you'd get in trouble for it. If they robbed me, I felt like I'd just had sex for nothing and had earned myself a beating. I'd have to come up with some other plan to make that money back before Rocco found out.

One time, I was almost brutally raped. The man took me to a vacant building and tried to attack me. Luckily, another man nearby heard me screaming, "Help!" and he came and helped me. I could have died.

PART 1:
Online Exploitation: The Facts

In recent years, we have seen a documented increase in the sale of exploited individuals through online venues of prostitution. For example, a 2012 news article on Syracuse.com reported that police in Syracuse, New York, had estimated that 90 percent of the city's prostitution trade had moved online between 2009 and 2011.[1] A 2011 research study found that 88 percent of the sex buyers who were interviewed had purchased women and children for sexual use via internet-advertised escort agencies, strip clubs, gentlemen's clubs, brothels, and massage parlors.[2]

The internet becomes a virtual red-light district where sex buyers can select and rent an individual for sex with the click of a button. It is a deviant expression of "online shopping." Just as you might pick a Netflix movie, a john can select the kind of woman he wants based on race, age, color, and physical attributes. The Internet plays a crucial role in validating the norms, cultures, and beliefs of a sex buyer's subculture as language developed in online chat rooms and on bulletin boards starts to normalize sexual exploitation. Due to the cultural stigma of the words "johns" or "tricks," online sex buyers refer to themselves as "mongers," "trollers," or "hobbyists." Internet prostitution has been called a "portal into the sex trafficking industry for vulnerable girls."[3]

The Trail of Online Porn

Discussing online prostitution requires us to look at the correlation between the evidential increase of online pornography use and the increase of online exploitation. In his book, *The Johns: Sex for Sale and the Men Who Buy It*, author Victor Malarek writes, "Porn and johns go hand in hand. Porn is what often turns the men on, revs up their sex drive, and sends them out into the night."[4]

The internet pornography industry continues to grow. A few telling facts:

- Every month pornography sites receive more regular traffic than Netflix, Amazon, & Twitter combined.

- At least 30 percent of all data transferred across the internet is porn-related.[5]

- Thirty-five percent of all internet downloads are porn-related.[6]

Intervention Manual

- Globally, porn is a $97 billion industry. At present, between $10 and $12 billion of that comes from the United States.[7]

As the use of online pornography continues to increase, we see exploitation taking new forms. For example, a sex buyer might 1) look at free pornography downloads; 2) then be offered hardcore pornography for purchase; and then 3) see a pop-up advertisement for prostitution in his zip code.[8] Moreover, when the high from the dopamine (chemical in the brain controlling the reward and pleasure centers) a man gets from renting hardcore pornography no longer satisfies him, voyeurism can turn physical, this time with a human being used as a masturbation receptacle. The demand for online pornography thus paves the way for online prostitution demand.

The Dangers of Online Prostitution

Online prostitution provides greater security for pimps and johns, but the exploited women remain at risk. PhD Melissa Farley, founding director of the national non-governmental organization Prostitution Research and Education, explains, *"By enabling men to evade arrest for soliciting prostitution, since they can remain hidden, indoors, and anonymous, the Internet is sex buyer-friendly. Its anonymity has created a private environment in which it is possible to engage in prostitution with a lower risk of arrest, fewer legal penalties, and less public exposure."*[9]

"The privacy associated with websites such as Backpage.com appeals to men who otherwise wouldn't risk approaching a woman on a street corner," says Randy Flood, therapist and director of the Men's Resource Center of West Michigan.[10]

In general, prostitution is a dangerous life for anyone, especially women. A study published in the *American Journal of Epidemiology* found the mortality rate of women in prostitution to be 200 times higher than the general population.[11] Additionally, a mortality survey of some 1,600 women in prostitution in the United States noted that murder accounted for 50 percent of the deaths of women in prostitution.[12] The sexual service is most often violent, degrading and abusive, including slashing women with razor blades; sex between a buyer and several women; tying women to bedposts and lashing them until they bleed; biting their breasts; burning them with cigarettes; cutting the arms, legs, and genital areas; and urinating and defecating on women.[13]

While the dangers of street prostitution are more obvious, sex purchased online exposes a woman to risks of a different nature. In their article, *"Online Prostitution and Trafficking,"* Farley and her two co-authors write, *"Because online sex businesses are less visible to the public, victims of sexual exploitation in prostitution are isolated and can be in greater danger from sex buyers."*[14]

Survivor and author Rachel Moran describes how meeting a sex buyer over the internet or phone removed her "street-wise" senses. She also argues that "screening" potential clients isn't always a viable option for women in online prostitution:

"To arrive at the home or hotel room of a man you have never met with a fixed idea in your mind as to how he is liable to behave when you are alone is one of the most dangerous things a woman in prostitution can do. I found it tremendously frustrating and risky to continually be in the situation where I couldn't use my senses to filter the men who would and would not use my body ... I had simply to rely on the attitude and tone of voice of the man on the other end of the phone."[15]

Additional pressures women face from being marketed and sold through internet prostitution run high, particularly because sex buyers can review a woman's "performance" online. While allegedly serving as community discussion forums, public message boards aimed at sex buyers (hobbyists) and women in prostitution (providers) are in fact sites where reviews of women in prostitution are posted and where prostitution is facilitated. Consequences from negative message board reviews happen rapidly, usually resulting in decreased earnings. To keep a buyer from posting judgmental, nasty reviews, women feel pressured to act as if they enjoy the rape-like sex of prostitution.[16] Those women who perform acts of prostitution in such a way that they convince sex buyers they truly enjoy the sex of prostitution, or who permit the buyer to rationalize his behavior, are praised for providing a 'girlfriend experience.'"[17,18]

What Sites Advertise Prostitution?

By 2010, revenue from Craigslist, a U.S.-based website featuring classified advertisements, was estimated at $122 million. Approximately 33 percent of this value came from prostitution-based advertising on the site's "Adult" section.[19] After experiencing extreme pressure from anti-prostitution advocates and lobbyists, Craigslist eventually shut down its Adult section in 2010. However, much of the traffic immediately transferred to similar classified sites such as Backpage, which has since become the primary site for advertising prostitution online.

Backpage.com Is Sued and CEO Arrested

In 2012, Erik Bauer, a criminal justice attorney based in Washington, established a nationwide, precedent-setting case on behalf of several minor girls who were trafficked on Backpage.com—what Bauer calls "the nation's largest human trafficking website." Bauer convinced the Washington State Supreme Court that the victims should be allowed to sue Backpage for the website's complicity in enabling illegal content to be posted and advertising multiple underage girls who were being trafficked for sex. The case will proceed to trial with a jury.

Bauer was asked, "If Backpage were forced to close its exploitative Adult section, would the online ads just transfer to another website, similar to what happened with Craigslist?"

Said Bauer: *"Then we'd go after that site too, and the next site and any others, and not stop until laws are passed that prevent these sites from acting as pimps and enabling kids to be sold for sex through their ads. It's disgraceful, and it has to change."*

In October 2016 the CEO of Backpage, Carl Ferrer, was arrested in Houston, Texas, and charged with pimping a minor, pimping, and conspiracy to commit pimping. Two controlling shareholders of Backpage were also charged with conspiracy to commit pimping. The site was described as "an unlawful online brothel." The investigation was partly prompted by reports from the National Center for

Missing and Exploited Children and thousands of instances of child sex trafficking through Backpage.

About Backpage:

- Although the Backpage site offers classified sales apart from sexual services, the vast majority of ads are listed under its Adult section. In February 2011, Backpage and five similar sites were estimated to generate annual revenue of $37.3 million from the sale of prostitution-linked ads.[20]

- In 2013, of the nearly $45 million generated annually by prostitution-based online advertising, Backpage accounted for 82 percent of the overall revenue, making it the leading publisher of these types of ads.[21]

- The *Seattle Times* quoted a city police officer who, in 2011, estimated that 80 percent of the young women investigated for prostitution in his area were advertised on Backpage.[22]

- A year later, in 2012, *The New York Times* quoted a trafficking survivor: *"For a website like Backpage to make $22 million off our backs, it's like going back to slave times."*[23]

- Backpage offers classified ads in 600 cities and in 30 countries and territories, including the United States, Canada, Australia, Ireland, New Zealand, the United Kingdom, the Caribbean, Mexico, and 12 countries in Europe, South America, and Asia.

About Backpage Ads:

- In early 2015, MasterCard and Visa pulled their card services from all transactions tied to Backpage's Adult section. As a result, more than 800 arrests have been made since 2009 connected to the site's adult service ads. Fifty of the arrests were for sex trafficking, involuntary servitude, or promoting prostitution.[24] Since then, Backpage has not charged to post ads in its Adult section, charging only for upgrading the post (for example, keeping the ad near the top). The site now accepts digital currencies like Bitcoin, Litecoin, and Dogecoin.

- The age range of those advertised through Backpage is 18 to 60 years old with the average age in the mid-20s. Different

> *"For a website to make $22 million off our backs, it's like going back to slave times."*
> **–The New York Times**

Example of a Backpage disclaimer.

ethnicities, body shapes, and experiences ("fetish," "girlfriend," etc.) are advertised.

- Typical ads include a photo, personal description, age, location, pseudonym, and phone number.

- Sometimes a disclaimer advises that the monetary exchange is "strictly for time and companionship only," and anything more is between "two consenting adults." In this case, the escort service is presented as separate from prostitution, but in reality, few men will pay money purely for companionship without the understanding that sexual services are included as part of his "donation."

- Ads can be linked to other ads for different girls connected by the same username or payment transaction. This kind of connection suggests that multiple women are being sold together, possibly through the same pimp.

- Developing literacy for the language and terminology in Backpage ads can be extremely helpful in intervention:

  > "In-call" means a woman will receive the buyer at her location, such as a hotel; "out-call" means she will go to his house or location of choice.

  > "Roses" is sometimes used in place of "dollars" when prices are stated.

  > "Specials" refer to discount offers for time/acts (a $60 special for 15 minutes). Many women refuse to offer specials. However, buyers will often try to barter down prices over the phone.

  > "Vanilla Daddy" implies older white men preferred.

  > "Fetish friendly" refers to fetishized sex acts commonly focusing on inanimate objects (such as silk gloves) or non-genital body parts (pregnant girl, feet-smelling, etc.).

  > "Dominatrix" alludes to BDSM (role play involving bondage, dominance/submission and sadomasochism).

  > "Two-girl specials" are often advertised, meaning two girls work together to offer threesomes or lesbian sex acts.

Online Intervention

> "Visiting this city," "passing through," or "new in town" imply that a girl is being moved by her pimp across state borders and may only be in town for a few days.

> "Our girls," "a variety of women," or "escorting agency" implies that an agency rather than an individual manages the ad.

> "Well-reviewed" refers to past john's reviews available on other escorting websites. A girl may have a separate profile on another website.

> "No AA" means "No African-American males." This is code for, "I have a pimp so don't mess with me or try to recruit me."

> "Young, petite" can mean they are underage.

Examples of Backpage Ads:

In addition to classified sites, many other websites, commonly promoted or referred to as "escorting sites," are designed to facilitate the sale of women for sex. Each woman has her own online profile including photos, a personal description, sex acts she will perform, and links to any reviews.

On many classified sites, the Adult section lists multiple options: escorting, body rubs, transgender, phone sex, and dominatrix.

Wiki Sex Guide

The Wiki Sex Guide (wikisexguide.com) is a self-described "sex buyer's global guide"—a detailed Wikipedia-style database written by

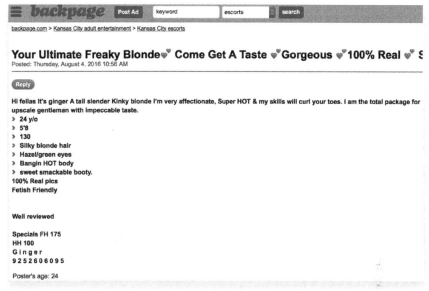

Example Backpage ads.

johns for johns. It outlines where to buy sexual services in each city across the world, including listings (addresses and phone numbers) and descriptions of erotic massage parlors, strip clubs, brothels, red-light districts, and prostitution tracks. It is gnarly and nauseating to read as an outreach worker; however, it is also extremely useful as all the research has been done for us. We highly recommend you use it to research your own city.

> *Days prior to this manual going to print, Backpage censored its Adult section, shortly after a U.S. Senate report released showing how Backpage hides criminal activity by deleting key terms from ads that indicate sex trafficking, including children. While this would seem to be a momentary victory, we know the war against online commercial sexual exploitation is far from over. We suggest you use the same texting methods to reach out to women on escorting sites, such as: Eros, Skip The Games, Escort-ads, USA Sex Guide, Erotic Monkey, Adult Search, Onebackpage, City of Love, Eccie, Stripper Web, Harlot Hub, Adult Look, Escort Fish, Escort Directory, Bedpage and others.*

Online Intervention

PART 2:
Online Outreach

Due to its demand-and-supply nature, while online prostitution exists, it will arguably never go underground. Pimps know that johns must be able to easily access the women they want to purchase for sex. Here's the good news: If the johns can find the women, then so can we. If the johns can easily contact the women online, then so can we.

In this changing landscape of exploitation, it's important for us to adapt to effectively reach the American-born and international girls who are being sold and trafficked through these online venues.

While law enforcement officials are increasing their efforts to catch and charge pimps, traffickers, and sex buyers through online stings, we can also leverage the open access of the internet to reach out and contact the women being exploited, cultivate relationships with them, and then support them on their journey toward freedom and healing. (For a highly recommended resource on online prostitution, check out Melissa Farley's 2014 document, "Online Prostitution and Trafficking" found on her website www.prostitutionresearch.com.)

Beyond the Photo

The women you will meet in real life are usually very different from their persona portrayed online. The language and photos in these profiles are meant to shout the message, "I'm independent! I love sex work! I am a nymphomaniac who loves the money, and I want to be doing this!" It is often a complete facade.

The typical woman behind the photo is just surviving: a single mom despairing over her perceived lack of options; a young runaway dependent on her pimp whom she believes truly loves and protects her; or a girl who has been sexually abused for years and feels nothing but shame and low self-esteem.

These women are daughters, sisters, and mothers, all made in the image of God. He has a plan and destiny for each of these women. He created them with an incredible purpose.

When viewing an ad (disclaimer: the ads are often semi-nude and highly sexual in nature), ask yourself these questions to help you pick up indicators about her situation as your group begins to do online outreaches:

> *"If the johns can find the women, then so can we."*

> Where was the photo taken? A house? A hotel? A local park? A professional studio? Some girls have a history in pornography exploitation, and sometimes professional photos aren't even the real person.

> Who is taking the picture? Is she (selfie)? A professional? A girlfriend? A pimp? Sometimes the person taking the photo can be seen in a glass or mirror reflection.

> Are multiple girls advertised together? Her profile may be linked to other girls' profiles.

> What can you note about her physical appearance? Are there visible bruises or scars? Are there dark shadows under her eyes? Is she possibly under the influence of drugs/alcohol?

> Is her face fully visible or blurred out? This can sometimes hint at how long a girl has been exploited, or her level of complicity. Often, a woman who is new to the industry blurs her face, but after several months or years, she stops caring and reveals it.

> Google search her number to trace past ads and different locations. She might have another website with a profile.

> The ad's photos and language can imply varying levels of exploitation. Remember that every woman is worth reaching out to. Sometimes the ones who seem the most complicit are actually desperate to get out.

Asking these questions and noting all available information prior to a meeting with a victim will give you insight into what questions you might ask her when you meet face to face. This information might also provide clues into the necessity for additional safety measures. Be aware that sometimes pimps or agency managers are actually creating and posting the ads and receiving the calls to manage the in-calls/out-calls. If the clues imply a strong presence of a pimp, you may need to heighten normal security measures. (We explain group intervention in detail in Section 4.)

As you familiarize yourself with the online community of these sites and other classified sites, you'll gain deeper insight into how it operates and grow in confidence when connecting to the women on it.

Texting Outreaches

Most online ads include a contact number at the bottom. Women frequently receive texts from potential sex buyers and throughout the day are accessing their phones. Texting a victim directly allows us to make first contact through a less-intimidating method than a cold-contact phone call. It gives her personal space and time to reflect on the text and respond when she feels comfortable. Texting women with ads on Backpage can initially feel awkward and unnatural, but remember that texting strangers and then meeting with them are completely normal for the person you're reaching. Texting is a modern form of outreach that can be an extremely effective way to arrange a meeting. We always text from an app, rather than our personal number, for further security. We recommend downloading Google Voice, Text Free or Text Plus. (See appendix for more details.)

Three possible ways to start a texting conversation:

1. **Hi (name), if you want out, there are people who can help you. Text me, (your name).**

2. **My name is (your name). I'm with a small non-profit called (name) and we connect with women in the industry to give them a gift of a beauty bag with makeup as a way to bless you. (Also a Walmart giftcard of $50) and a list of local resources and services. We just want women to know they have local support. Myself and one other volunteer would meet you at a local fast food restaurant. Are you interested and are you available today/tomorrow?**

3. **Hey is this (name)?** (This approach will generally cause her to respond right away, and she may be more likely to reply to future texts after she has acknowledged you've texted the correct person. Once you're in a texting conversation, inform her of the information above.)

In a texting conversation (**only ask questions after she is already engaging with you** in an open way), consider asking her questions:

> What's your biggest dream?

> Do you have any kids?

> Is this your hometown or are you just here visiting?

> Are you interested in receiving information about local resources? Is there anything you're in urgent need of right now?

Intervention Manual

Extra Tips

- When choosing an outreach team name, if possible, try to avoid a name that would be patronizing to her, explicitly connected with "rescue," or overly religious.

- Remember that the main action step is to secure a meeting with her, preferably that same day. Don't risk making her suspicious by asking too many in-depth questions about her situation over texts. Some questions can be saved for the face-to-face meeting.

- Avoid overly patronizing language, such as, "You have so much potential. You're better than this," or "How can you keep doing this?"

- Avoid using lingo like you've been in the game (if you haven't) as it could be insulting to victims.

- Use smiley faces (emojis and text characters) to keep the tone relaxed and friendly.

- Be aware that it may be a pimp who is actually responding to the texts. That is why it is imperative to speak on the phone with a victim before meeting in person. You want to hear the girl's voice.

- If you arrange a meeting, be sure to set a clear location, address, and time.

- If you're meeting the following day, call or text her that day to confirm the meeting/remind her in case she forgets. Afternoons are generally better than mornings.

- Only meet in public places! We recommend meeting at a well-known fast food restaurant chain, like McDonald's. You'll feel safer and so will she.

- Follow up with her even if you don't end up arranging a meeting. If you have a significant call/texting conversation, follow up in a few days and let her know you're still there for her and that a gift is hers if she'd like it. Consider also leaving her with the National Trafficking Hotline number (or text line).

- Consider putting up a free and simple website or ministry Facebook page (with no photos of you or links to anyone's personal Facebook) with a picture of the bag and an email address). It may reduce suspicion if there is a legitimate website you can point her to. It also opens up an additional line through which she could contact you.

- Consider placing an ad on one of these websites, offering resources/assistance/support with your hotline number attached so women who wish to know more can reach out. The ad may get deleted though.

For examples of actual text conversations that can be used to effectively connect with exploited women, see Appendix A: Texting Scripts.

Carrying Your Heart Through Texting Outreaches

For anyone involved in texting outreaches, facilitating a worshipful and missional environment is vital. Only female team members should be looking at online ads, and all team members should be aware that the images in prostitution ads online are often highly sexualized and graphic images, including:

- up close shots of body parts

- little clothing or nudity

- implied sex positions

- generally graphic content

As you go through the ads, be aware of the lies the images are shouting. As we said earlier, you'll find that the real individual is vastly different in nature from the image portrayed in the photo.

Ask yourself questions that might help you get to the heart of the matter. What false messages are these images telling? Replace any lies you discern with God's truth. Remind yourself of truths such as, "I know that women are fearfully and wonderfully made in the image of God" and "Every woman is a daughter with a purpose and identity."

For texting outreaches, we suggest you:

> Stay in group settings only.

> Pray before and after.

> Play worship music in the background.

> Dialogue with the Holy Spirit throughout the texting outreach.

> Imagine Jesus sitting beside you. Know that He is with you as you send these texts.

> Take comfort knowing that Jesus already holds each one of these women in His hand. He sees the entirety of their exploitation.

> Pray for every face you see, even if it's a five-second prayer: "Jesus, You love this daughter. Break in and set her free!"

> Allow yourself to feel the compassion or righteous anger of Christ. Know that it's okay to cry during or after outreaches. Your tears are precious and powerful.

> After each texting outreach, verbally process the emotions you experience (especially on initial ventures) with another team member.

Finish the texting outreach by praying together for the women you contact and for your teammates. Speak the name of Jesus over your team and leave any burdens or toxic thoughts/emotions at the foot of the cross. If you have a burden for this issue, be confident that God will give you the grace and discernment to do the work He's calling you to do.

Tri-Teams

To ensure stability for the exploited individual, as well as members of the intervention team, we use the tri-team system relational structure. Only three members on the team (plus a security detail) will be in a relationship with one exploited individual for the duration of the outreach. This system allows a woman to build long-term trust and form relationships with a core team rather than navigating a revolving door of new people.

Tri-team members are chosen by team leadership and selected according to their availability/capacity.

Tri-Team Roles

Primary: The team member in the primary role is usually the first to establish initial contact with the individual and is the primary source for bonding and establishing trust. The team member in the primary role is the only one who:

- texts/calls an exploited individual to build a relationship
- sets up meetings

- follows up with ongoing contact

- completes all history and contact forms

Secondary: In the secondary role, the team member supports the primary role:

- accompanying her to meetings

- being a familiar face to the individual

- being available to assist with the practical needs if more than one person is require

- completing forms after each meeting

- providing prayerful and emotional support to the primary team member

If the exploited individual requests additional contacts, the secondary can provide a Google Voice number (see Appendix B) and establish a phone relationship to supplement the relationship the primary team member has already established.

Third (on-call): If the primary or secondary team members are not available to attend a meeting, the third team member is the assigned back-up member to go along to meetings and give support. The person in the third role should be informed of relational developments to support the primary and secondary team members in personal prayer and to intercede in prayer for the exploited individual.

The Security Detail

A male team member isn't on an actual tri-team, but he will be present as a security detail at every initial meet up with an individual, but he should drive separately (discreetly in the background if you're meeting at a public location) and at future meetings if necessary (for example, if a pimp will likely be nearby).

Private details of the exploited individual's circumstances are confidential within the tri-team and security, a policy that gives team members permission to discuss and process her story. Within this relational structure, you can discuss questions, frustrations, offenses,

Intervention Manual

and burdens regarding the individual you're reaching out to and contending for in prayer.

Also, team members should remain accountable and vulnerable with one another about the personal impact of this specific case and the need for prayer. It is vital that team members are debriefing, processing, and walking through this journey together with the emotional and prayerful support from fellow team members.

Practically, the capacity for each intervention team member is limited by realistic time and emotional requirements. Therefore, we've set parameters on the level of engagement that we believe is spiritually, emotionally, and physically healthy: Each team member may only serve in the primary role for two individuals, and the maximum number of individuals a team member may be working with at any given time is three.

Some Examples of Tri-Team Involvement:

- Primary for one girl and secondary for two girls.

- Primary for one girl, secondary for one girl, and a third (on-call) for one girl.

- Primary for two girls and a third for one.

The same three team members don't always need to serve on a team together. While the team working with one individual remains consistent, team members may work on various tri-teams composed of different support members. If an individual has not been in contact with you for three months, her status on the database will be set to "inactive," and you're released to initiate and take on new relationships.

The diagram below illustrates how the three roles work together:

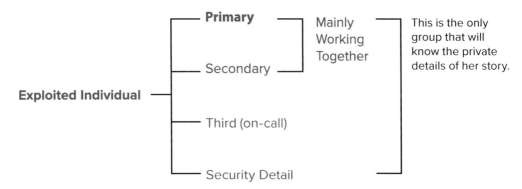

Online Outreach for Male Team Members

EPIK is an organization that trains men to reach out to sex buyers, combating trafficking at the root: demand. Volunteers place fake online ads on sites like Backpage.com and receive the texts and calls from the flood of johns immediately responding to the ads. They warn and counsel the buyers who are at the point of purchasing a girl for sex (so they think) of the consequences of their illegal actions and offer resources and programs for those struggling with deviant behavior and sex addiction. EPIK functions as a highly trained and sophisticated neighborhood watch program as they provide law enforcement with specific information related to the illegal activity of prostitution to assist them in their efforts to also combat sex trafficking.

For more information about EPIK and how to train a group of male volunteers in your community, see www.epikproject.org.

Exodus Cry Team Testimony: Abbie

These women have just as much to offer me as I have to offer them.

When I first heard about human trafficking as a young girl, my heart was gripped with a burden to minister to exploited individuals. I didn't know what that would mean, but I definitely had a romantic vision related to the role I would somehow play in whisking these women away from the tragedies of their lives. When I joined the intervention team, my perspective changed drastically.

Working in intervention tempered my zeal in a healthy way. I suddenly became very small and much less of a hero when I finally understood that I knew nothing of the tragedies of these women's lives. They didn't need to be rescued; they needed to be empowered by love to finally make choices of their own. The dignity of choice is a sacred and beautiful thing, and it is something these women have lost.

Being part of the intervention team has been as much about me learning to love as it has been about these women learning to receive love. I have learned what it is to restore, not rescue. One of the most important things I have come to learn is that these women have just as much to offer me as I have to offer them. They have offered me vulnerability and trust, exposing deep places of brokenness and hurt. I have yet to encounter anything as beautiful as a woman opening her heart when it has been closed for so long.

The Value of a Gift

"A gift opens the way..." (Prov. 18:16).

One of our core values of outreach is offering a gift. We bring gift bags to every exploited individual we meet with on outreaches, whether it's on the streets, in a strip club, or at a meeting from a texting outreach. A gift bag (or other gift such as roses) immediately makes a girl feel special and valued and sets a highly positive tone to the relational dynamic. It also serves as an icebreaker. The first five minutes of a face-to-face meeting are often spent with the girl exploring the gift bag and talking about the items in it.

Exodus Cry gift bag

When texting a girl, we always tell her that we want to bless her with a free gift bag full of beauty products and essentials. We also inform her that we would love to talk about life options too, but there is no pressure and the gift comes with no strings attached (See Appendix A: Texting Scripts).

Securing donations of gift bag items is also a great opportunity to involve local community members and organizations that have a heart for girls caught in sexual exploitation but aren't part of the intervention team.

Suggested gift bag items include

- shampoo
- conditioner
- feminine pads
- tampons
- soaps
- toothpaste
- toothbrushes
- Band-Aids
- dental floss
- makeup (lipstick, lip gloss, mascara, blush, eyeliner)
- perfume
- compact mirror
- nail polish and nail kit
- facewipes
- hairbrush
- hair accessories
- socks
- gloves
- jewelry
- candle
- a small Bible
- a journal
- a devotional book
- a non-perishable snack
- a copy of the "Father's Love Letter" (for a copy, see the website fathersloveletter.com)
- a non-patronizing note of support
- We suggest gift bags to strip clubs include less hygiene products (e.g. toothbrushes, floss, Band-aAids etc) and more makeup products. Save the hygiene products for the street bags as there is often a greater need.

> We strongly advise you to use unused/unopened gifts only. If you wouldn't give it to a friend as a gift, reconsider including it in the Hope Bag. We always want the women to feel loved, blessed and excited by the gifts.

Online Intervention

PART 3:
Building Relationships

As we've already established, rescue isn't just a one-time event; it's a journey and a process. The success and sustained impact of intervention lies in the building of relationships—supporting an individual during each step of her courageous exit out of exploitation. At Exodus Cry, we view ministry to exploited individuals less as traditional evangelism and more as a friendship rooted in trust, investment, and support. Similar to our personal friendships, real trust takes time to develop. Our relationships with these men and women will unfold naturally. We must surrender that process to the Lord, knowing that as we demonstrate His unconditional, compassionate love, He will reveal Himself and open up opportunities to share the gospel in the context of an established relationship. Below, we share practical suggestions for showing and sharing the love of God to exploited individuals.

Follow Up

During the first face-to-face meeting with an exploited individual, keep in mind that a primary goal is to follow up and continue building the relationship. Ask questions that show her you've remembered details she may have shared with you (for example, "How is your daughter Emma doing?"). If she shares any personal or family information with you, it indicates she trusts you. Other suggestions:

- Let the conversation flow organically and allow authentic friendship to develop. You want the time you spend together to feel fun, open, and practical.

- She may be in need of groceries or clothes, so be prepared to offer to help with those, if your team is able.

- At the end of the meeting, consider ways to arrange a second meeting within the following week and keep in touch via text.

Introducing God

Although valuable, the practical solutions for addressing basic needs and improvements for an exploited individual fall short of the holistic restoration of life to body, soul, and spirit. Jesus is the ultimate solution and provider of true justice and freedom. Recognize that the battle in the war on sex trafficking is first and foremost a spiritual one. We contend for a heavenly breakthrough and solution to an

> "I never look at the masses as my responsibility; I look at the individual. Maybe if I didn't pick up that one person, I wouldn't have picked up 42,000 ... The same thing goes for you, the same thing in your family, the same thing in your church, your community. Just begin—one, one, one."
>
> —**Mother Theresa**

individual's needs through prayer—for the light of Christ to invade and overcome the darkness. We always want to point an individual to the source of true healing and breakthrough: Jesus Christ.

"For though we live in the world, we do not wage war as the world does. The weapons we fight with are not the weapons of the world. On the contrary, they have divine power to demolish strongholds. We demolish arguments and every pretension that sets itself up against the knowledge of God, and we take captive every thought to make it obedient to Christ" (2 Cor. 10:3-5).

At the end of each meeting, you might offer a prayer of blessing. By praying for her, you're inviting the presence of the Lord to minister to her—providing a glimpse of what communicating with Jesus looks like. She shouldn't feel pressured to respond. Instead, the goal is for her to leave the meeting feeling supported and encouraged. Avoid bringing up Jesus too much in the first few meetings, as it will come over as though you have a religious agenda. Let trust be built first!

As she sees the life you live out before her, God will naturally come up in conversation. Often, she'll be the one asking questions. Time and again during this process, we have seen closed hearts open to the Lord. After establishing an authentic relationship with her, you can feel freer to share your testimony, invite her to visit a church or event, or pray with her to follow Christ if she wants to and is ready. At this stage, as her relationship with the Lord grows, it is important to facilitate and encourage her dependence on God over her co-dependence on you.

Celebrating the Individual

In the parable of the Prodigal Son (Luke 15), the jubilant father calls for a banquet party to celebrate the return of his runaway son. We want to embody this same spirit by celebrating every step of an exploited individual's journey home.

Make a point to rejoice with her over significant markers and achievements that elevate her and her progress. Here are some examples:

> When she lands a job or gets into a course, take her out for a special meal.

> If she's pregnant or becomes pregnant, throw her a baby shower. Often, pregnancy can be a catalyst to a girl exiting the life. A baby can be a wake-up call and an additional motivator to leave exploitation for her child's sake, if not her own.

> Take her to a Mother's Day event.

> Make a special event of buying her first Bible or a new pair of shoes!

> Celebrate her birthday.

> Enjoy a special meal to celebrate a one-year anniversary of your first meeting.

> Consider hosting a large, celebratory banquet for all of the girls your team has connected with.

> Celebrate the small things and improvements, e.g., "Last month you wouldn't have even noticed this—I'm so proud of you!"

We have the honor of affirming (with words and actions) an exploited individual's worth and value, showing her that she is loved and special in both our eyes and God's.

An Opportunity for the Church

Here is also a beautiful opportunity for your church(es) to give additional support to your team and offer assistance. Within the body of Christ is an army! Is there a dentist at your church who does pro bono work? A businessman willing to take a chance on a new employee? A life coach or tutor? A small group for new moms? A lawyer who could give advice? Be sensitive to how to best involve your church if everyone immediately knows the girl is a victim of commercial sexual exploitation and swamps her as she arrives at a service, this could be terrifying for her.

Protect her identity and story wherever possible, while still involving the body of Christ. We offer our love and support, but know that ultimately we are not responsible for their lives or choices and we have to accept that. Accept that even when it's a challenge. We are not the savior! It is also completely acceptable to place firmer boundaries or draw back from a relationship that becomes dangerous for you or exploitative on her side. (For example, she begins to ask you to give her money for her bills each month, but you suspect there are drugs involved.)

Love That Goes the Distance

As you may have already learned or will soon discover, ministry to exploited individuals is a crucible of love. Our motives and agendas are tested, and our best efforts to love are consistently refined and challenged. Time and time again, we surrender our weak and broken love—love that gets frustrated, disillusioned, and disappointed—in exchange for God's far-reaching and long-suffering love. The "love" chapter (1 Corinthians 13) in Scripture gives us a clear picture:

"Love suffers long and is kind; love does not envy; love does not parade itself, is not puffed up; does not behave rudely, does not seek its own, is not provoked, thinks no evil; does not rejoice in iniquity, but rejoices in the truth; bears all things, believes all things hopes all things, endures all things. Love never fails" (1 Cor. 13:4-8).

We must also remain committed to reaching for this kind of love and continue loving those that the Lord entrusts to us, even when it's difficult. We love them when they use us for money or convenience. We love them when they stand us up. We love them when they lie to us. We love them when they make unwise or destructive choices. We love them when they fight against us or reject our efforts to help them. We love them when they take a step forward and then two steps back. We should not be shocked by their choices; this is the life they know. We love them right where they are, in the midst of their messy journey, and we demonstrate to them the kind of love that perseveres and continues to believe in them.

Other tips:

> Try to avoid giving her money. A pimp will likely take it. Keep a stack of giftcards for different purposes (Subway, Ross, Applebees, Walmart). You could do a fundraising gift card drive or apply for free gift cards from Target, etc. (if the ministry is part of a church/non-profit).

> Be prepared for these women to not be ready to leave the life, or to come out of exploitation only to go back to their pimp again. This can be particularly hard after you've loved them and invested in them. It is vital to be prepared for the heartbreak that can come with working with exploited people.

> Validate her feelings—how hard it is to start over, how scary it can be to navigate the unknown, etc.

Remember to always seek wisdom regarding timing. When do you persevere and remain fully available, and when do you back off and give her space?

There are often times where it is imperative to present various options or lifelines but then leave the ball in her court and let her initiate follow-up contact. In this way, you are laying your agenda aside and giving her the dignity of taking full ownership and responsibility over her process. We've seen this dynamic at work with many exploited individuals and have also come to expect ebb and flow in the relationship. For example, if she chooses to pull away and not return your texts, you must let her. Sometimes love looks like backing off. Text her from time to time, letting her know you're still here for her and that you care for her. When she is ready or when a crisis hits, she'll feel safe reaching out to you again, and you'll be there. In the meantime, pray for her, trusting in the Lord's timing and the story He is writing for and through her life.

Trans-Theoretical Model of Change

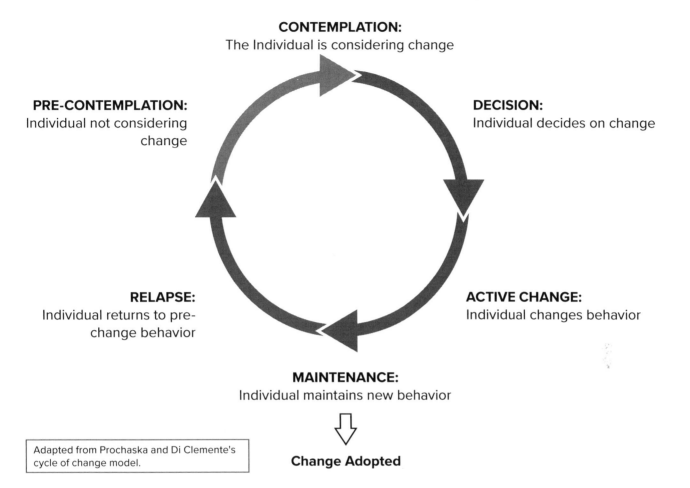

Adapted from Prochaska and Di Clemente's cycle of change model.

Exodus Cry Team Testimony: Denise

Over the past seven years, my husband and I have offered our time and home to help prostituted women in difficult situations. We have witnessed how circumstances and injustices in the life of a human being can prevent them from walking out their God-given destinies and how God calls us to be ministers of the broken-hearted. We have realized that we were created to help others find their freedom from bondage and walk in the integrity of Christ with joy!

One would think, *love is the easy part*. Although in some ways love is simple, I've found it also to be costly. There is a sacrifice to be made. As we are the expression of Christ's sacrificial love, we too must lay down our lives for the broken, the needy, the poor in spirit.

Once we learn to love as Christ loved, we can feed His sheep. We will need to be filled with this love and the word of God to feed His sheep good food.

On my journey in this ministry, I've come to understand that love is about being the servant of all as an expression of Christ. He has taught me how to love without bounds. Unconditional love is sometimes tough, however, as 1 Corinthians states "...faith, hope, love, these three, but the greatest of these is LOVE."

Online Intervention

TESTIMONY
From Death to Life: Ruby's Story

As a teenager, Ruby was a ward of the state and often got into trouble with the police for her rebellious behavior. When she was 15, Ruby ran away from home with a man who offered her a place to stay in another state. She recognizes him now as her pimp—the man who introduced her to the life. She can clearly remember the first time he presented her with a condom and told her to sleep with another man while money was exchanged. Over the next eight years, Ruby was prostituted in several states, often alongside other girls.

Our intervention team met Ruby through a texting outreach. In the context of our weekly team meeting, we split into small groups to pray over girls we were reaching out to. We began praying for Ruby, and as we prayed, we sent her a text introducing ourselves and offering a free gift bag. She responded immediately, expressing interest in meeting us that week to talk and receive a gift bag.

My teammate and I (Helen) met Ruby in a McDonald's downtown and bought her a coffee. We had no idea what to expect, but Ruby seemed relaxed and grateful for the gift bag we gave her. She was tall, with platinum-blonde hair and grey-blue eyes. We spent over an hour talking with her as she opened up to us about her life. She expressed a desire to come out of exploitation and start a medical course at a local college. That course gave us a good connection point for a second meeting. We began to see Ruby more frequently, helping her apply and arrange interviews at the local college.

When praying for Ruby, we felt the Lord wanted us to speak out the phrase, "Lazarus, come forth!"—the very words that resurrected a dead man from the grave. Lazarus emerged from a tomb of darkness and decay, out into the sunlight, with the promise of a second chance to live. We knew Jesus wanted us to release this same cry over Ruby's spirit and so, in prayer during those weeks, we consistently called her forth. Years of exploitation and disassociation had made Ruby seem numb and lifeless on the inside. But we knew that Jesus had a cup of life-giving water waiting for her at the well of encounter.

Suddenly, a series of circumstances found Ruby in crisis. She reached out to us, knowing we were people she could trust. Pregnant, broke, betrayed by her boyfriend, and without a car or home, she needed our help. We provided some short-term accommodations and then,

Intervention Manual

in answer to prayer, some of her relatives in another state invited her to move in with them. So we helped Ruby and her young child pack all of their belongings and leave Kansas City to be in a safe place. It was a rushed goodbye, but we knew the Lord had intervened. This was the beginning of a new start for Ruby. We had come alongside her at the right time.

Ruby soon found herself attending church with her relatives. She loved it and told me excitedly that she was "getting in touch with God." It wasn't long before Ruby gave her life fully to the Lord and decided to get baptized, both she and her oldest child. What a picture of death unto new life, a Lazarus coming forth out of the grave into the saving embrace of Jesus! A few months later, she gave birth to her beautiful and healthy baby, displaying yet another powerful image of hope and new life.

We have noticed that the Lord often places us in these girls' lives right before they enter a crisis situation. Having built trust, we are then the ones they turn to, and we are able to offer them the help they need.

One Sunday, a year later, my teammate and I attended church with Ruby and her young kids. The prayers during the service that week happened to focus on girls trapped in sex trafficking. Tears rolled down our faces as we witnessed Ruby, standing beside us, raising her hands, and whispering, "Jesus, save these girls." After the service, we asked her oldest child what his Sunday school lesson was. He replied: "Jesus raising Lazarus from the dead."

A Q & A with Ruby

Ruby shared with us about her life before encountering God, the relationship she now has with Him, and the message she would give to girls who are living a life of exploitation.

How has your life changed since we first met you?

Ruby: Meeting y'all made me really think about things. I already had a serious plan to put that lifestyle behind me; I just hadn't yet. Meeting you guys came at just the right time. God had been working on me for a while. He helped me see everything from a different perspective. My car getting stolen and everything leading up to me leaving Kansas City … it all happened at the right time and in the right place.

My life now is so much less hectic and more relaxed. I have the same income now as I did then, but I'm less stressed because I have faith in God and I trust Him. And I just want you to know how grateful I am for you guys. I couldn't have gotten here without y'all. I'm glad I felt I could open up to y'all. You were definitely angel-sent.

How has your relationship with God grown?

Ruby: I'd always "prayed" to God, but I never knew how to really pray. I just prayed when I needed something. Now I pray all of the time—when I'm thankful or just thinking! It's more about a relationship now. I pray with my family, and I read the Word every day. I'm trying to read five chapters every day, and each morning, I pray Psalm 91 over my kids and me. I would say I have a relationship with God that I never had before. It's exciting … more and more every day. Instead of dreading tomorrow, I'm excited for the future. I wake up wondering what God has in store for me today.

I'm just so happy with where I'm going. Jesus is working on me every day. He's working on my heart. Every day is exciting. My sadness went to happiness. God forgave me, and I've forgiven myself.

What is something that has been hard since leaving the life?

Ruby: During that time [of being trafficked], the devil tortured me. Even now he pokes at me—tells me to go back to that life. I just pray, "Lord, get these thoughts out of my head!" I'm not ever going back to that life.

If you could give a message to girls still in exploitation, what would it be?

Ruby: My message to girls still in the life is that they don't have to be! They don't have to do that. They can get out. I used to think the only way to survive was doing that, but it wasn't. I thought there wasn't a way out, but I came out—cold turkey! I'd tell these girls to just have faith in God. There's a way out of everything. Pray and get a relationship with God; He's the answer to everything.

In Her Shoes: Using Art to Fight Injustice

"Throughout history, creative storytelling has raised awareness about important social issues and inspired people to take action."
— Benjamin Nolot, founder and CEO of Exodus Cry

"We need stories that incite us to greatness." — Storyteller, and TEDx speaker S.J. Murray

There's something so poignantly symbolic, yet simple and accessible, about shoes. We all walk in them; they are our vehicles for carrying us on our journey. While they are often functional, shoes simultaneously express something unique about our personality.

As an artist, I (Helen) am passionate about art that powerfully conveys a message or a story. As part of the Exodus Cry intervention team, I wanted to combine my love for art with my love for these precious women to produce paintings around the theme of prostitution. I hoped to highlight individual stories but with the intent of inspiring hope rather than being overly harrowing given the seriousness of the subject matter.

One day, while praying for ideas, I felt drawn to look at my annual planner. On the front cover was an image of an empty pair of women's shoes. I was so arrested by this confronting image that it evoked questions of the identity of the original wearer and the story behind these intriguing, well-worn shoes.

As I looked at my planner, I was inspired to do a series of paintings. During the transatlantic slave-trade era, slaves were bought and sold with weighty shackles chained around their ankles. Women exploited through the sex industry today are not always sold with physical chains; however, psychological and spiritual bondage entraps them. Many feel there is no way out. Coercion from pimps, cultural systems, and lies about their own worth keep women locked inside the sex trade. Most women trapped in prostitution want to escape but believe they have no other option for survival. Though the physical chains are largely absent in this modern slave trade, there is one very visible and recognizable symbol of slavery fastened around the ankles of sexually exploited women: stiletto-heeled shoes. Their shoes are intertwined and associated with their exploitation.

The paintings feature "working" shoes from the girls I have met and

Online Intervention

journeyed with on their road from slavery into freedom. Each piece of art champions a trophy of grace—the abandoned chains of captives set free. Each painting is uniquely personal to each woman's story, yet it is anonymous and non-sensational and does not expose her.

When our intervention team at Exodus Cry enters an exploited girl's life, we come alongside her. We don't drag her from the front, push her from behind, or project our own choices or dreams onto her.

We lay aside our own agendas, determined not to steal the dignity of her choice. We purpose to walk beside her in friendship, let her discover her own dreams and desires, and support and empower her at each stage along the way. She makes the choice to walk forward into her destiny.

After a girl has made significant steps towards her own liberation and when I have established trust with her, I ask her if she would like to exchange the pair of her old "shackles" for a pair of brand-new shoes. It is a symbolic act, marking the beginning of a new journey and a new identity. We shop at the mall together, and she picks out a special pair of new shoes. It's the "Cinderella moment" of leaving the rags behind and putting on the glass slippers. One woman chose a pair of Coach pumps, and I couldn't help but think of the Cinderella parallel. Two other women chose Air Jordan sneakers, worlds apart from the stilettos they'd exchanged.

I'm reminded of another story. In Jesus' parable of the Prodigal Son, when the son returns home, the father runs out to him, embraces him, throws a homecoming party to celebrate, and gives his boy a new pair of shoes.

I titled the painting series "In Her Shoes." Each piece is meant to encourage us not to judge but to be stirred with compassion by the plight of each woman, seeing her as a sister—to consider her pain and her journey—and to rejoice at her courageous decision to leave a life of exploitation. The shackles are gone! The tomb is empty, and a new life awaits.

 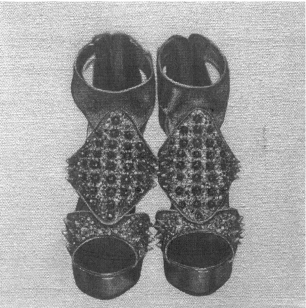

The Young Man's Story

Recently I (Helen) was sharing about sex trafficking at a seminar, and I had displayed the various pairs of stiletto shoes on the stage while I spoke.

Afterwards, a young man approached me. He looked distressed.

"I found the talk extremely difficult to sit through. I need to confess to you that I used to buy women in prostitution due to a severe pornography addiction. I have so much shame and I want to repent. Will you pray for me to receive God's mercy?"

Slightly lost for words, I wondered if it might be more appropriate for a male to pray with him instead. But then I looked into his earnest eyes and recognized the courage it took for him to make this confession to me, especially knowing the work I am involved in.

So I prayed for the young man, pronouncing the forgiveness of Jesus over his life and calling him into victory in the violent battle against lust. We talked for a while and then he left. A few minutes later he returned, his own shoes in hand.

"If the girls' shoes symbolize their broken chains, can I give you mine?"

He quietly walked over to the stage and placed his shoes by the others.

That night he walked away knowing he was a free man, his own shackles of sin and shame left at the cross. In that moment, I remembered an interview from an ex-trafficker named Ohad—in our documentary, *Nefarious*. He aptly summed it up this way: "I was a captive of one thing, she was a captive of another thing, but God wants to set the captives free."

Each pair of shoes in this project tells a story of a real life that was touched and transformed, serving as a visible reminder that, one by one, God is setting the captives free. Our prayer, in intervention at Exodus Cry, is for more empty shoes that once belonged to sons and daughters who have now been liberated from the shackles of exploitation.

SECTION 3:
Street, Strip Club, and Jail Outreach

70 — A Day in the Life: Pimped: Vanessa's Story (part 3)

72 — Pimp Tactics 101

PART 1
75 — Street Outreach

PART 2
84 — Strip Club Outreach

PART 3
87 — Outreach to Jails

90 — A Brief Encounter: Monica's Story

A DAY IN THE LIFE
Pimped: Vanessa's Story (pt. 3)
[Trigger warning]

A trafficked girl's relationship with her pimp represents an intensely complex web of physical and psychological coercion, manipulation, dominance, and fear tactics. The goal of a pimp is to obtain complete control over his victim's mind, body, and soul. Told in her own words, Vanessa describes her relationship with her pimp.

I tried to escape from the brothel house twice before I was rescued. The first time I ran, I got beat really bad. Rocco told me if I ran again, I would lose privileges of a car and my phone. The second time I tried to escape, I got farther than I did the first time. Each time, he found me. The second time I tried to escape he told me, "I will kill your daughter in front of you if you run again." I never tried running again. Later, I discovered he was tracking me through my phone.

I definitely didn't talk back to Rocco 'cause he had actually killed one girl. He was mad at her and put a lot of drugs into her system. He shoved her, she fell to the ground and hit a table. She was knocked out, and she died on the spot. He put a needle in her arm and tried to make it look like she overdosed on drugs, but he meant to kill her. One time he beat this girl and cracked her forehead. I remember him grabbing me by my throat, pinning me against the wall, and choking me 'til I couldn't breathe.

> *"He had sex with all of us girls. He was cruel, disgusting ... his eyes had flames in them."*

I didn't ask questions 'cause when you asked questions you got in trouble, or you'd say something wrong and get punished. He knew everybody; he was friends with high people. He even had lawyers and cops working for him. He was the boss, running this world. He was the boss of the city.

He had sex with all of us girls. He was cruel, disgusting ... his eyes had flames in them. He would film everyone that he slept with [to make pornography]. We had to act like we enjoyed it or he would make us redo it until he got off. It was mean, nasty. We had to call him "Baby," which made me sick.

Lucy, the girl who trained me, fell in love with him. She's still at the house and has been there for a long time. She kind of has to love him, y'know, to survive. He says he loves her too, but he doesn't. That's not love.

Rocco would make us take the Molly pill before we'd go on a call. It's pretty much like a date rape drug. We would be so strung out on it that we wouldn't even care or be fully aware that we were having sex. You feel really out of control when you're on it. When the effect wears off, you feel intensely depressed, like you need it [again] to make your body feel better. You get addicted.

He had three underage girls when I was there. Every girl who had kids at the house had only girls. It was like he recruited girls who had just girls. It was like he was waiting for us to be done and our daughters to grow up.

My 17-year-old cousin was in foster care. She had gone through a lot. She was sexually and physically abused. One day she emailed me saying, "I need a place to stay." Rocco read all of our emails and made me show him her picture. He said, "I want her, and you're going to get her." He wanted me to recruit and train her like Lucy had trained me. He wanted me to do that to my own flesh and blood. My heart was crushed.

If I keep remembering [what he's done to me], I won't be able to live my life freely. I don't want it to keep me from doing things. I'm not going to live my life in fear every time I turn around. I don't want to raise my daughter in a life of fear. I refuse to.

Street, Strip Club, and Jail Outreach

Pimp Tactics 101: What Vanessa's Story Tells Us

If a trafficked girl has access to a car or other seemingly tangible opportunities to escape a brothel, people sometimes fail to recognize her as a slave. Surely, they think, she could easily run away? They wrongly conclude that she must be choosing to stay in that life.

Vanessa's experience illustrates the diverse reasons why a woman might stay with her captor:

Fear of consequential punishment: Very early on, a pimp instills monumental fear of what will happen to his victim or her family if she attempts to escape. Many traffickers and pimps like Rocco are linked to mafia members or people in "high places." By surrounding themselves with those who cover for them or who are willing to turn a blind eye, pimps are often able to continue operating in their crimes with brazen assurance that they won't be stopped. Projecting this image of power and high-level connectedness is another tactic pimps and traffickers use to eradicate any hope that leaders in "the system" would help an exploited woman or be on her side.

Emotional and sexual exploitation of victims: As Vanessa shares, a pimp will regularly have sex with the girls he enslaves—another means of exerting dominance over his victims and reminding them they are his property, while simultaneously using them for his own perverted pleasure. Some girls bond deeply with their captors and believe they're in love with them. Called Stockholm syndrome, this carefully crafted, distorted, emotional loyalty is another reason a girl might remain with her pimp.

Drug addiction: The introduction of addictive drugs is another powerful method that pimps use to keep a girl dependent on him. These drugs are also used to stimulate her libido, increasing her ability to receptively have sex with multiple men per night without being fully conscious of all her body is enduring.

In addition, although the pimp or trafficker (the exploiter) primarily uses violence, deceit, manipulation, and drugs under his control, the bond the girl feels with an exploiter is real and not casually broken.

PIMP TACTICS 101

Guerilla Pimp

Uses: force (kidnapping, violence, drugs, blackmail) to overpower prey.

Target Prey: Teens at a party, the mall, on social media … anywhere lacking responsible supervision.

"Come party with me."

"Don't tell anyone where you're going." "If you don't do what I say, I'll post these (naked or embarrassing) pictures of you all over the internet."

What to Watch For: Men 18+ who hang with younger girls. Overly friendly girls (recruiters) who persistently invite other teens to party and drink/do drugs with them.

Romeo Pimp

Uses: charm, gifts, and flattery to romance prey.

Target Prey: Girls looking for love or acceptance. Runaways. Sweet and naive young men and women.

"I love you." "Nobody else understands me." "I'll give you everything you deserve." "I can't live without you." "Dream with me."

What to Watch For: Guys who fall in love too quickly. Guys or girls (recruiters) who encourage teens to run away from home, promising a happier life.

CEO Pimp

Uses: money and business strategies to swindle prey.

Target Prey: Aspiring models and entertainers, especially naive young women away from home.

"I'm an agent. You have what it takes to make it in this industry. Trust me." "This is strictly business." "I can make you rich." "Fill out this form." (personal information)

What to Watch For: Men who flash cash and promise stardom. "Agents" who are too pushy. "Agents" who want bikini or "artistically nude" photos.

Victim

Intimidation and Threats: Pimp "breaks" the victim by letting her know he's dangerous—beating, raping, yelling, showing weapons, etc. He threatens to hurt her and her loved ones.

Control and Isolation: Pimp keeps the victim close and makes her dependent by calling constantly, moving her in, taking money away, monitoring her moves, etc.

Psychological Manipulation: Pimp acts friendly sometimes, apologizes after abuse, promises that things will get better, calls victims "family," makes victim think she's damaged goods and is purposed for a life of trafficking.

*www.SowersEducationGroup.com

Street, Strip Club, and Jail Outreach

The excerpt below from author Rachel Lloyd's memoir *Girls Like Us: Fighting for a World Where Girls Are Not for Sale* reveals these strongholds:

"Very few bad relationships are all bad. The same man who used to both physically and emotionally abuse me was the same man who would give me a pedicure and carefully paint my toenails—the same man who would make me the most elaborate breakfasts in bed, clean the house, make me laugh harder than anyone else could. If there had been nothing good, I wouldn't have stayed. Even most girls' relationships with pimps, while defined as they are by economic gain and forms of slavery, have elements that are 'normal.' Incidences of violence are juxtaposed with the day-to-day realities for everyday life: cooking, eating, sleeping, watching television. Even being put out on the track becomes so normalized, so numbing, that it's hard for most girls to view this as abuse.

"It's just what you're expected to do, another part of a regular day. Viewing pimps as one-dimensional monsters isn't that helpful in terms of understanding the girls' experiences. While the acts that pimps have committed are heinous and deserving of full punishment under the law, overlooking the humanness that the girls surely see only makes it harder to understand why they stay or, especially, why they go back. We understand that women in domestic violence relationships don't necessarily want the relationship to end. They just want the abuse to stop. It's what keeps the cycle going, the belief that this time it will be different, that he'll change, that you can get the good parts back, without any of the bad parts intruding this time ..."

Traffickers are often seeking new investments and are all too aware of an increasing demand for younger, underage girls. They see the women they sell as business commodities, producing for them a very high profit in a billion-dollar industry. As Dan Allender, PhD, explains in the DVD resource *Nefarious: Merchant of Souls*, "[A pimp thinks], if I sell a line of cocaine, I sell it one time. If I sell a woman, I get seven-plus years' work out of her."

> *"Viewing pimps as one-dimensional monsters isn't that helpful in terms of understanding the girls' experiences."*
> —**Rachel Lloyd, in her memoir,** *Girls Like Us*

PART 1:
Street Outreach

Commercial sexual exploitation occurs in numerous different venues across many cultures. Prostitution occurring at the street level is less common in the United States than in other cultures, but it is still just as perilous. Due to the nature of soliciting buyers directly on the street and getting into their car to be taken to an unknown location, victims of street prostitution face unique dangers. Many exploited individuals are met with untold violence and uncertainty. With each exchange for sex, their lives are at stake.

In addition to the violence that men and women face at the hands of johns, an individual can incur a long-lasting criminal record as they receive police citations for solicitation (or traffickers forcing them to hold guns, take drugs, or recruit others which can lead to co-conspirator charges), ultimately leading to jail time.

Sadly, a growing number of transgendered persons are being exploited as well, as many are rejected by their families and driven to the streets. Finding employment and social services can be difficult, making them even more vulnerable to sexual exploitation.

Understanding Life on the Streets

Regardless of what we see with our eyes, to effectively reach out we need to understand several dynamics about the streets and the men and women who are sold for sex there. Most importantly, we must remember that each exploited individual has a voice and a unique story about his or her entry into the commercial sex industry and why he or she is still there.

Most of the individuals sold on the street are under third-party control. Although you may never see the pimp or the person controlling them, a third party is almost always involved. The third party could be a pimp, a drug-addicted boyfriend, or someone who collects a fee in exchange for "permission" to stand on the corner. A third party is anyone who profits from the avails of prostitution.

Most victims view their trafficker or pimp as a familial "daddy," or believe they're in a romantic relationship with him (it is advisable to "mirror" what she calls him (i.e. her boyfriend) and only refer to him as her "trafficker" or "pimp" after she comes out of the life and you have built a strong relationship with her). They might speak of the relationship in purely positive terms, but as outreach workers, we

Street, Strip Club, and Jail Outreach

must be aware of the language and lifestyle of exploitation to understand what could be happening in their lives beneath the surface. Sadly, drug addiction can often be a strong controlling factor that perpetuates the cycle of exploitation for men and women in street prostitution.

Preparation for Outreach

Direct outreach to the vulnerable must be an overflow and an extension of a life of prayer. In street outreach, we go to the areas in our cities that are often suffering from poverty, violence, and neglect. We place ourselves in these areas to reach out to the sexually exploited and to pray for the transformation of these communities and the families that live there. We also pray that the cycles of poverty, drug addiction, sexual abuse, and exploitation would be broken.

Before embarking on a street outreach, meet together as a team for a time of worship and prayer, confessing your sins and attitudes or heart postures that could leave a door open for spiritual attack or distraction. Put on the "armor" of God (Ephesians 6) and pray for covering and protection for your team and the individuals you'll encounter. Then as you go into the impacted area, pray prayers of life and destiny over the area and the individuals you meet. If every crack house on the street were merely shut down, the neighborhood would be left with boarded-up, neglected homes. Instead, we desire transformation—for the power of Heaven to invade this area and make all things new. Pray for families to move into these neighborhoods, for the establishment of legitimate businesses, and for the chains of bondage to be broken.

As you head to the streets, continue in a spirit of prayer, talking to Jesus about how He feels about the men and women you meet.

During the Outreach

Below, we outline the protocol for approaching the streets:

- Drive through these areas and if you see an individual, pass him or her, pull over to park, and then get out and walk to meet him or her. Avoid immediately pulling over when you see someone. Put yourself in their shoes. If you were walking on the street and saw a car suddenly pull over and a group get out and approach you, you'd be scared! Give the people you want to reach enough time and space to see you approach. Sometimes, groups will simply park and walk the whole street if the weather is good. It's up to the team leader to make this decision. You move more slowly, but you also have more time to pray over the area.

- Assign a driver for the night. The driver must always be thinking about the next step. Always park and wait in a well-lit area—no driveways and no one-way or dead-end streets. Make checking mirrors, watching alertly, and praying for the team second nature. Make sure the car is always close and in a position to drive away swiftly.

- Always stay together. This is a non-negotiable! Never proceed anywhere alone. Do not go around any corners without the entire team and the security detail watching where you're heading. Be aware of your surroundings and the whereabouts of your team members. Be on guard for one another. Even when you're praying for a person, be aware of what's happening around you. Is the person looking around? Are people approaching?

- Move and be led by the Spirit as a team. This is not a one-man show. The choices you make affect your teammates. Communicate with team leaders any impressions you're getting and wait for their direction before taking action.

Team Roles for Street Outreach

Team Leaders: The team leader will decide what areas the team will target, who will approach each man or woman you meet, and when the outreach is over. Team leaders should be vocal and proactive in communicating with the team; don't assume the team is automatically staying alert and aware to the situation. The team leader is also responsible for keeping records of what occurred on the outreach, the people the team interacted with, and any services the team offered.

Female team members: Because women are perceived as less threatening, we always ask female team leaders to initially approach the prostituted individuals. They can begin the conversation and offer a gift as an icebreaker. Our goal is to always relationally connect with each exploited woman or man we meet. A five-minute encounter on the street can be good. But if she spends too long talking to us, she may get into trouble with her pimp because she's unable to meet the required nightly (monetary) quota. So we need to be sensitive and discerning.

Male team members: The men on your team are there to minister alongside female team members, and they play a critical role in the safety of the team. After female team members have approached the exploited individual and made sure that he or she is comfortable, men are welcome to step in and engage with the individual. However, they should continue to be alert to the surroundings and keep an eye out for approaching individuals or cars.

If you do run into a situation with a pimp or other threatening individual that appears to be escalating or making team members uncomfortable, use the ATM principle to diffuse the situation as quickly as possible:

- A: Ask him, "Can you please back up?"

- T: Tell him, "Back up."

- M: Make him: "You leave."

You may not always go through the entire process of ATM. Use discernment.

Absolutely no weapons are allowed in an outreach environment. This includes concealed weapons. If anyone on your team is unwilling to abide by this and wants to conceal as they go on outreach, then they are not welcomed and should not be on the team.

Approaching Exploited Individuals

First, remember that anyone you approach on the street is "working." Although we don't legitimize prostitution as work, we respect the individual and honor his or her wishes. Many want to be left alone, and others might feel like they're in danger if they talk to us. This is their territory, and we are just visiting. They will have to pay the consequences of our presence more than we will, so we want to respect and give them space if they're unwilling to talk to us. We also never want to interfere with any interaction with johns. It is important to bear in mind that the exploited individual may have a nightly (monetary) quota their pimp requires from them. She may get into trouble with the pimp if she spends too long talking to us, so we need to be sensitive and discerning.

As you approach someone, explain who you are and what your purpose is for being there, letting them know you care about their well-being, and listing available services to exploited persons. Assure them that when they are ready, you're available to assist them. Make sure to offer him or her a gift bag. Consider including a contact card with a vague, non-"escape" sounding email, or your Google Voice number (or the National Trafficking Hotline Number) could be presented in a subtle way e.g. a hot pink business card, designed to look like it could just belong to her friend and NOT an anti-trafficking organization. Or the number could be subtly hidden as the bar code number on the side of a lipstick case.

You can expect a wide range of emotions and reactions. Many will be uninterested and distant; others will want to tell you their life story. Be present with them and convey a spirit of love. Below, we've listed helpful guidelines:

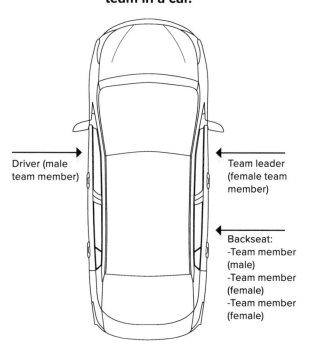

Example of a hypothetical team in a car.

Driver (male team member)

Team leader (female team member)

Backseat:
-Team member (male)
-Team member (female)
-Team member (female)

- If you are going out in groups of five (two males, three females), the team leader should decide ahead of time who will approach each individual and who should start the conversation. Only three (two females, one male) should approach each individual (and the other two should remain in the car praying).

- Look at their eyes and not their bodies. Let them know your desire and ability to help them.

- Make sure you smile! This is simple. But the intensity of the streets can make people uneasy and on guard, and they forget to smile. As you smile and show them that you're kind and comfortable around them, they will begin to feel more at ease.

- Be cautious about physically touching these these men and women in an overly familiar way. Often, we can begin to chum around with someone and hug them or touch their arm, but during outreach to exploited individuals these gestures are inappropriate.

- If you have a good conversation and want to give them a hug or lay hands on them for prayer, ask permission first.

- Pay attention to their non-verbal cues. Watch their body language and eye contact. Be sensitive to things going on around you that may be less obvious: Are they in danger? Are their eyes darting after every car that drives by? Is he/she being watched? Is a client approaching?

- Be open as you talk to them. Ask the Lord to show you the way He feels about this son/daughter. Look at their eyes and listen to them with that perspective.

- As they begin to be more open in their conversation, ask questions. Get to know them.

- While one teammate is talking, the others (particularly the male) should be looking around and watching for pimps and johns. Be safe and smart.

Approaching Transgendered Individuals

Transgender is an umbrella term used to describe people with a gender identity and/or gender expression different from their sex assigned at birth. The expressions of a transgender identity could range from cross-dressing, to taking hormones, to having a sex-change operation.

Transgendered young people end up in prostitution because of vulnerability, often due to the stigma placed upon them as a trans-person; rejection from family that drives them to the streets; or difficulties in finding employment. In desperation, many turn to prostitution to survive. As with more traditional prostitution, the same elements of force, fraud, and coercion can sometimes be present in the exploitation of a transgendered person. The added stigmas surrounding transgendersim often only enforce the isolation of exploitation. Additionally, fewer services cater specifically to this population, so finding adequate referrals can be more challenging.

This population is among the most rejected and misunderstood, and therefore we must respond with the deepest love and compassion towards them. We must always ask God for His heart towards this individual. We have seen many transgendered exploited individuals dramatically encounter Jesus and experience the love of God in beautiful and powerful ways.

We recommend you research services in the city beforehand that offer resources and services specifically for this population, as well as emergency and non-emergency housing options that would receive them (if this is something desired by them).

As with anyone we meet on the streets and in the sex industry, exchange numbers to stay in touch where possible!

Offering Services

Always check with the team leader before offering immediate physical assistance or help. If you have a very personal connection with the exploited individual and want to leave secure, personal contact information, you can do that as well. We recommend using Google Voice as a platform to protect your personal contact information but still allow for relational development that is genuine (see Appendix B).

It is not always possible on street outreaches, but we want to be prepared to follow up with and build relationships with individuals outside of the ministry/street setting. This could be coffee the next day, taking them to job interviews, helping with legal assistance, etc. For direct, one-on-one ministry, follow the same procedures as online outreach (outlined in Section 2), forming a tri-team, including a male security detail who will follow the two female team members for the first meeting. If the individual expresses needs for professional services such as housing, connect him or her with the proper person on your team. Particularly if you are the team leader, be prepared ahead of time with local resources and options if the individual should express interest or need!

Dos and Don'ts for Street Outreach

- Don't ever give out money in an outreach setting. On the streets, you will likely be approached by all kinds of people who may be panhandling or in need. While we want to be prayerful and help those in need, these requests can often be distractions from the main focus of our outreach.

- When praying for the individual at the end of the conversation, keep your eyes open, not closed.

- Do leave money and all valuables behind at the office or at home. Bring a copy of your ID to have on you at all times.

- Don't give out personal contact information. Instead, leave them with either your Google Voice number or the National Trafficking Hotline (presented in a very hidden or subtle way so that if found, the pimp would not suspect she is trying to escape!). National Trafficking Hotline number: 1-888-373-3888.

- Most importantly, don't make promises you aren't able to keep.

PART 2:
Strip Club Outreach

Strip clubs, also called "gentlemen's clubs," are found in most cities across the United States. Typically, the building's windows are blacked out or boarded up, and neon signs are common advertisements. For many women, strip clubs become a gateway into prostitution, where personal boundaries are tested and they're introduced to the sex trade. Not all dancers are bought for sex, however sex does often take place either in back rooms at the club or at a meeting in a second location (such as a nearby hotel) arranged after a lap dance. We classify all forms of the sex trade (prostitution, pornography, and stripping) as exploitation and a form of violence against women.

In outreaches to strip clubs, our goals are:

- To bless the women with a free gift

- To let them know they are valuable and special

- To build relationship and trust with them and the club

- To leave some kind of contact (hotline number, email, website) for a woman to contact you if she wants to reach out

Preparation

- Like street outreach and meetings (texting intervention), we highly recommend you take gift bags (or simple gifts such as roses) to the strip clubs as your "reason" for going in and interacting with the women. Gifts clearly state the purpose for entry: to bless the women. Without gifts, your motives for being there could be questioned.`

- The brighter and bolder the gifts bags, the better (e.g. hot pink or lime green). Rather than taking the inconspicuous black Hope drawstring bags we give to women when we meet with them from texting outreaches or on the street, you'll want to use smaller, paper gift bags with pretty tissue wrapping for the clubs. A bag like this is obviously a fun/innocent gift and can be clearly checked out by club bouncers without raising suspicion. We also recommend offering gifts to the bouncers (king-size chocolate bars, soda, etc.). They are the gatekeepers to the club, and building positive rapport with them is essential.

- In terms of intervention teams, we recommend smaller teams (two to three women and one to two guys remaining outside as security) unless you have built a relationship with the club bouncers/managers and they're okay with you bringing in more team members.

- We suggest that male team members approach the club with the female team members and be introduced, but stay outside the club or in the entrance. During this time, these team members can be interceding for the female team members or building relationship with (and ideally even witnessing to) the bouncers.

- Going on a less busy night (such as a weekday) will give you greater chance of getting in.

During the Outreach

- Approach bouncers confidently with a smile! Say something along the lines of, "Hi! We are a group of friends who put together some gift bags for the ladies to let them know they are valuable and special! They've got makeup and candy in them. We'd love to hand one to each person. Would that be okay?"

- Some groups believe it's more respectful to call a club in advance and ask permission to come, however in our experience, showing up at the club with brightly colored gift bags and seeking permission at the door is more effective. Seeing you in person, bouncers/club owners are more likely to be receptive and to let you in.

- If the bouncer refuses to let you in, ask to leave the gifts at the club for the women. On your second visit, ask to enter and if they still refuse, call and ask permission from the owner/manager.

- If the bouncers let you in, ask to be introduced to the manager so that he can see you in person. Once you have the manager's blessing, you know you will always be given future entry into the club.

- Especially during your first few visits, as you're building relationships with the women, don't spend too long with any of them. You may get complaints that you're taking time away from the ladies' work.

- You may be invited or be given permission to give gifts to the women in the dressing room who are on a break (although in most strip clubs this is not allowed), but we suggest that you don't ask to go backstage on your initial visit. Instead, build trust and rapport with the club first. Once you're backstage, you may have more opportunities to talk longer and offer prayer. The women are often more relaxed backstage than when they are in work mode on the club floor.

- We recommend all male team members approach the club with the females (and hold gifts so it is clear they are with the female team members). However, they should remain outside the club, interceding for the women and chatting with the bouncer (and offering him prayer where possible!). We would never take our male volunteers into the clubs with us because a) topless women will be dancing and b) the clubs are less dangerous than the streets for volunteers and the males' role as security and intercessors are best placed outside.

- Also, note that team members under 21 would not be able to enter clubs.

Additional Ideas for Strip Club Outreach:

- Place a prayer request box in the dressing room (with permission and after you've built relationship).

- Offer to decorate the club dressing room and backstage areas.

- Offer to throw the women a luncheon or party in the club or at a nearby location.

- Plan special seasonal outreaches for Valentine's Day, Thanksgiving, Christmas, etc.

- Take home-cooked meals, cookies, or cakes to the women, bouncers, and club managers.

- For additional in-depth training on strip club outreach, see Harmony Dust's organization Treasures' website www.iamatreasure.com for information and resources.

> *"We classify all forms of the sex trade (prostitution, pornography, and stripping) as exploitation and a form of violence against women."*

PART 3:
Outreach to Jails

When thinking about alternate and effective ways to locate exploited individuals, we realized that jails, correctional facilities, prisons, and juvenile detention centers are all prime places to consider for outreaches.

In the United States prostitution is still illegal, so those in prostitution can be can be charged and placed in jail for soliciting. Crimes related to the lifestyle on the streets can also warrant incarceration. While we strongly disagree with criminalizing and arresting prostituted people and we advocate for the law to change, we recognize that God can use that time they have away from everything and they will often reflect and seek change during this time.

Christina Rangel, founder of Extreme Love Anti-Trafficking and trafficking survivor-leader, was put in prison for crimes her trafficker coerced her into doing. In prison, she had a dramatic encounter with Jesus that changed her life forever. Her story, among others, inspired us to start doing outreach in a local jail.

Because jails are away from the streets, pimps, abusive relationships, and drugs, and women are momentarily distanced from the chaos of the streets and exploitation, they offer a unique window of opportunity to reach women. Jails can become the "wilderness of encounter" (Hosea 2) where all is stripped away and we reach people in a crisis moment as they're re-evaluating their life.

In 2015, our team started partnering with the local jail's chaplaincy, delivering Bibles and daily devotionals to women who had requested them and teaching a 10-week Bible study curriculum we wrote, called *Free Inside*. It is our belief that, even when physically incarcerated, the women can encounter the true Deliverer and experience more freedom than they ever knew. Spiritual and psychological strongholds can keep them bound to sin, addiction, despair, and exploitation. Jesus declared in John 8:31-32, "If you hold to my teaching … you will know the truth and the truth will set you free." We want to teach the women the foundational truths of who Jesus is and invite them to encounter the Healer and Savior as the first step to their freedom.

Each Bible study topic is designed for women with a past of sexual abuse and exploitation. Topics include overcoming fear and shame, the cross, forgiveness, body image, sexuality, introduction to prayer/

the Bible, Jesus and women, etc. A significant percentage of the women who come through the program have a history of prostitution or exchanging sex for survival needs. Each woman receives a packet with information about local resources, services, partner programs, transitional living, and welcoming churches. We particularly try to identify those at high risk of returning to a pimp or exploitation.

At the end of each weekly session, we offer a prayer time and have led several women through inner healing, forgiveness prayers, breaking toxic soul ties, deliverance, and salvation. Many have encountered the presence and love of Jesus for the first time. As one woman told us, *"I feel like it was the mercy of God that He allowed me to be put in jail. I was headed for death on the streets, but He intervened and has saved my life."* After leading another girl through forgiving the man who first molested her, we saw her let in the healing love of Jesus: *"It's like I can feel my heart beating for the first time."*

We encourage your team to investigate opportunities to volunteer in your local jail, in partnership with the chaplaincy, as an additional effective way to reach exploited women at a key point in their journey.

Start by:

1) Contacting a local jail/juvenile detention center/prison and set up a meeting with the Christian chaplain.

2) Show the chaplain your curriculum/book/Bible study course plan to do with the women. (If you don't have one, contact intervention@exoduscry.com.)

3) The chaplain may say "no" to the course proposal, but may be open to you coming in as a chaplain's assistant (e.g. to help deliver Bibles and offer prayer etc.).

4) There may be other groups from churches already volunteering in the jail. Consider offering to connect with them or assist with their programs.

5) Be prepared to complete an application and obtain pastoral references, etc. Attending a jail training course may be required as well.

Exodus Cry Team Testimony: Jordanne

Though I've seen women encounter Jesus and be transformed through various avenues of outreach, I've never personally seen it as powerfully and consistently as in the *Free Inside* Bible study program we facilitate at our local county jail for women with a background of sexual abuse/exploitation.

Jesus is as strategic as He is relentless in His pursuit of our hearts. For many of the women, incarceration is the catalyst that brings them to the end of themselves and into His grace. Over and over, I've heard the same testimony: "God brought me here to give me a second chance."

Each week can be different in terms of numbers and faces, but what doesn't change is the raw hunger the women in the room possess. Like the woman in the Bible who had exhausted all her options for healing and desperately pressed through the crowd to touch the hem of Jesus' robe, their hunger incites an immediate response of God's Spirit.

It has been awe-inspiring for me to see different women receive the grace to forgive their abusers, boldly begin leading other women in their cell to the Lord, or simply say their first words to their Creator. Each week, my perception of God's love is challenged and expanded as I witness His grace fill the cracks and script the unique storyline of each woman. Jesus is transforming jail sentences into cords of loving kindness, drawing women into freedom on the inside.

TESTIMONY
A Brief Encounter: Monica's Story

In intervention, our desire is always to build a lasting relationship with an exploited individual—to walk out the journey into freedom alongside her. There are times, however, when we are only able to meet with someone once and then, for a number of reasons, we may never hear from her again. Perhaps she changed her number or was trafficked to another city. Perhaps she escaped and destroyed her phone to break all ties to the exploited life she lived. Often, we will never know.

When we reflect upon these one-time meetings, we can remain confident that God is able to use something as small as a 10-minute conversation to shift the course of a girl's life. For a brief moment in time, we enter into her world in a God-ordained encounter, sowing powerful seeds of truth and hope into her heart.

I (Helen) learned about Monica from a Backpage post during an online outreach and texted her, asking: "If you could get out of the life, would you?" She answered, "I escort because I have to. It's to survive and yes I want out. I want out bad." I was unable to secure a meeting with her that day; however, a few weeks later crisis hit and Monica discovered that she was pregnant by a client. She reached out to me, and we began talking on the phone. The Lord opened a window of opportunity for me to speak life and destiny into this young woman's life, to empower her choice to keep her baby, and to pray for her over the phone.

Through sobs, Monica told me, "I think God is giving me a chance to have a fresh start. I feel like I've been living in a black tunnel, but I see a light now. I want to move away from here and live with a family and have this baby. It could be a whole new chapter in my life." She told me she had contacted an adoption agency and had made arrangements to move in with a family out of state.

The night before her bus left Kansas City, Monica wanted to meet my teammate and me. We waited for her at a fast food restaurant for over an hour before we heard from her. From the rearview window, we saw a man drop her off and wait in a car in the parking lot. Monica was in her mid-20s, with dyed black hair and stained makeup. She looked wary and tense upon arrival but seemed moved and grateful to meet us. She was blessed by the timely beauty bag.

We probably only had 10 minutes with her before she needed to return to her ride. We embraced the opportunity, showered her with encouragement, and prayed for her before she left. She hugged us, and her dark eyes looked glassy as she said goodbye. Her text to us later said, "You are angels and a true blessing to have experienced. Thanks so much for your nonjudgmental generosity." A few days later, Monica's phone was disconnected and we have not heard from her since.

More than a year later, her number remains obsolete. We have not seen her post online since that time. We have no idea if the man who dropped her off at the restaurant was her pimp or whether he helped her get on the bus that night. Did she ever get to that family and have the baby? Did she go on to find the Lord? We don't know her story's progression, but we do know that the Lord used us as stepping stones toward Him to share simple words of hope and love and to bless this young woman in His name on a significant night in her life. Whether we enter these women's worlds for 10 minutes or 10 years, we count it as time to be the hands, feet, and eyes of Jesus for however long He places us beside them. His will is fulfilled when we minister to the one in front of us during those divinely orchestrated meetings. We can trust in His love that continues to pursue them long after our moments together are finished.

"We can remain confident that God is able to use something as small as a 10-minute conversation to shift the course of a girl's life."

Exodus Cry Team Testimony: Katie

[Katie and her husband served as a Safe Family for a trafficked girl as part of her restoration process]

The gospel became alive and real, playing out right before my eyes.

When Lilly came to us, she was broken and sick but also full of hope. I knew the main thing she needed was to feel welcomed and safe. The Lord told me to treat her as one of my own. That was easy. I knew how to do that. My main goal was not to correct all the wrong things in her life but to show her daily living connected to a Savior.

I asked the Lord for grace and small conversations that spoke of His love and strength. He supplied abundantly. We talked and prayed. Lilly was ready to receive all the Lord would give. That's not to say that fervent prayer and intercession didn't happen on her behalf. I prayed constantly for the Lord to have victory in her heart and mind.

Lilly gave her life to Jesus, and the Holy Spirit started working right away. She was a sponge soaking up the Word; I was just a conduit vessel He used.

We faced each challenging situation one at a time. I found that I was learning to trust in Jesus right along with her. Having this precious young mother and her child in my life has opened up a realm of glory I had never seen before. He changed me just as much as He changed her. The gospel came alive, playing out right before my eyes.

Minors

If you ever come across an exploited individual on outreach who tells you she is under 18, then she is a minor in commercial sexual exploitation.

The US Department of Justice outlines key steps to take:

- To report an incident or suspicious situation that may involve the prostitution of children, call the National Human Trafficking Resource Center (NHTRC) at 1-888-373-7888, or file a confidential online report at http://www.polarisproject.org/what-we-do/national-human-trafficking-hotline/report-a-tip. Your report will be forwarded to a law enforcement agency for investigation and action.
- To report an incident involving the sexual exploitation of children, file a report on the National Center for Missing & Exploited Children (NCMEC)'s website at www.cybertipline.com, or call 1-800-843-5678. Your report will be forwarded to a law enforcement agency for investigation and action.
- You may also wish to report the incident to federal, state, or local law enforcement personnel.

SECTION 4:
Intervention in Community

96
A Day in the Life: Rescued: Vanessa's Story (part 4)

PART 1
98
Building Sustainable Inreach and Outreach Communities

PART 2
103
Being Prepared: Researching an Exit Plan

PART 3
106
Imperative Security Measures

PART 4
111
Sexual Integrity

PART 5
116
Men in Outreach

121
Breakthrough by Prayer: Gabriella's Story

A DAY IN THE LIFE
Rescued: Vanessa's Story (pt. 4)

Vanessa courageously escaped her pimp and is now beginning to rebuild her life. Told in her own words, she describes her life now:

I can finally speak about my trafficking experience without crying. Even about the things that were terrifying at the time. After feeling silenced for years, it's time to speak out. In the past, if I ever tried to speak my mind about something, I'd get punished.

I still have a hard time making decisions about things, as my entire life I have never felt I had a choice. But now I'm able to choose. Even simple things like, "Where do you want to eat?" I'm not used to having those kinds of choices! I'm like, "I don't know, I don't care"… making choices feels weird. I'm still getting used to the freedom to make my own decisions about my life.

I moved in with this family after I was rescued, before I went into a program. They were amazing! This couple invited my daughter and me right into their family and was so loving to us. I'd never experienced anything like it. They were so kind and genuinely wanted to know how I was. They'd ask things like "How are you?" and "What would you like to do today?" They didn't try and control me. They even taught me how to read properly! They are so special—like a real mom and dad to me. I can tell the mom anything. If I were about to do something wrong right now, I could talk to her and know I wouldn't be judged. We could talk it through. I know I can call her anytime, and she'll talk to me. Or I could go over to her house. I'd never had that kind of bond with anyone before.

I was 98 pounds when I was rescued. Now I'm 127 pounds! I'm gaining weight, and I have muscles. My daughter can't push me over anymore! [laughs]. I'm stronger. I'm so proud that I can read now, and I've gone to college and have stayed in college! That was something I chose. I'm also learning how to be a better mom to my beautiful daughter. I feel I've achieved something, even in just one year. The fact that I can talk about everything now without crying shows me that I'm healing from the memories. I just want it all to be gone. It is gone [smiles].

Vanessa was in a restoration program for more than a year. To celebrate the one-year anniversary of her rescue, she threw a party inviting each individual who had played a key role on her journey to freedom: her

mentors, therapists, spiritual parents, the family she lived with, her social worker and other key individuals, friends and staff who love her and have encouraged her at each step.

It truly takes an army of people to come alongside one girl, with each team member offering the unique love and service they have to give. Vanessa's road toward healing and restoration requires the body of Christ to continue running alongside her and a team of unnamed heroes being Jesus to her in the process.

PART 1:
Building Sustainable Inreach and Outreach Communities

Now that you have a better understanding of the needs of the individuals you're reaching, we want to focus on building community. In our years of outreach to exploited persons, we've learned that the key factor in sustaining our hearts and our work is community. Because of the chaotic, violent, and degrading lifestyles these men and women are immersed in, they often have many needs and for a short time can become dependent upon you when they decide to exit the lifestyle. From detox services to the basics of shelter and food, to the aid of law enforcement, the needs can be endless. If you're not prepared and not surrounded by your own internal and external support system, trying to meet those needs could leave you physically burned out and emotionally exhausted.

Author Henri Nouwen wisely speaks of the reality of compassion in community in his must-read work, *Compassion: A Reflection on the Christian Life:*

"The message that comes to us in the New Testament is that the compassionate life is a life together. Compassion is not an individual character trait, a personal attitude, or a special talent, but a way of living together... When there is no community that can mediate between world needs and personal responses, the burden of the world can only be a crushing burden.

"When the pains of the world are presented to people who are already overwhelmed by the problems in their small circle of family or friends, how can we hope for a creative response? What we can expect is the opposite of compassion: numbness and anger ... The Christian community mediates between the suffering of the world and our individual responses to this suffering. Since the Christian community is the living presence of the mediating Christ, it enables us to be fully aware of the painful condition of the human family without being paralyzed by this awareness."

The Safety of Internal Community

As we come alongside exploited persons, offering them support and friendship while building trust with them, we must do this intervention within community. Internal community provides:

- A common set of visions and values to guide the team through the daily efforts of reaching exploited persons.

- Support. You can't do it all on your own. You need the help of other individuals. Their perspective, skills, and experiences help us best serve the men and women you're building relationships with.

- Prayer. Every time we make contact with an exploited person, we're entering into a spiritual battle. We must be covered in prayer, and as the body, we wage war against the spiritual strongholds that keep these individuals in bondage. Meeting for regular times of prayer as a community is vital.

- Compassion. As caretakers, we can often vicariously experience trauma from the things we see, hear, and experience while working with exploited men and women. We need compassionate and empathetic friends that understand and can rally around us in the moments of our exhaustion, heartbreak, and joy.

The Support of Tri-Team Community

As part of a tri-team, regularly praying in agreement and unity for the freedom of the person you're reaching out to can be a crucial and powerful tool for promoting a breakthrough in a person's circumstances. Tri-team community provides:

- Love with no agenda: In community, we hold each other accountable to silence the agendas that can often creep in and be projected onto the exploited persons we serve. Whether a girl goes back to her pimp, cuts us off from a relationship, or resists our assistance, walking together in internal community helps steady our hearts for the disappointments and heartbreaks.

- Love that stays: Many times, we'll be in relationship with one exploited person for months, sometimes years, while they continue to be prostituted or return to the life. Because we don't always see quick results, we must remind each other that love is patient, it goes the distance, and it doesn't easily walk away. Ultimately, love never fails. Scripture tells us we can't love like this apart from abiding in Jesus, the vine (John 15), the very source of life. We must do this in community where we're anchored by the support of our teammates and their prayers.

- Accountability and covering in relational support to victims: The tri-team community structure also helps prevent burnout and heaviness, offering comfort, encouragement, and empathy to one another in the lows as well as rejoicing together in the victories.

The Importance of External Community

If we're going to effectively reach and help exploited persons, we need an army! Victims often need education, healthcare, legal aid, and discipleship. Additionally, the process of coming out of this life can take a great amount of time and patience through many ups and downs.

To effectively empower victims with the courage to walk away from this life, we need to develop an extensive network of services and referral points. You can usually find local resources for the exploited through churches, government offices, law enforcement, public social services, and local businesses. An increasing number of people and organizations are willing and ready to get involved in assisting exploited persons. Educating people and organizations in our communities about the realities and challenges that victims face is mission critical. But remember that education must always come with an invitation to get involved and meet needs—body, mind, and spirit.

Engage Together created this excellent wheel, outlining the different community roles and areas required in order to bring freedom, restoration, and justice to victims of sex trafficking. (For more info go to www.engagetogether.com/freedomstrategy.)

Alliance for Freedom, Restoration, and Justice, Inc. Copyright 2017.

Intervention Manual

Steps to Building an Intervention Community

Building a sustainable community requires strong leadership, a thorough screening process, mutuality in commitment and shared values, and the freedom to make mistakes. Weekly times of prayer, biblical encouragement, and times for relationship building create a safe context for team members.

One caution as we jump in: Remember that you're always a student. Never be so locked into a specific approach and strategy that you're unwilling to change. As you learn what does and does not work in your community, consciously altering the plan and strategy is critical to longevity and sustainability. Always learn from those around you who have done it longer, have made mistakes, and have continued to show up!

Below, we outline the initial steps for building your outreach team:

Step 1: Open information meeting. Here, you want to explain the function, values, and commitment level required. You also want to share a clear vision and specific goals for this team. (We recommend you prepare the way so that you can focus less on education and more on building a team. In the weeks before, hold an educational workshop or invite a guest speaker.)

Step 2: Application process. After the meeting, ask interested attendees to take an application. The application outlines common questions to ask of potential team members and allows for an initial screening process for applicants. The application process requires two pastoral references and two interviews with your leadership.

Step 3: Interview process. Personal interviews with applicants allow for time to discuss, face-to-face, any questions or concerns that came up on the application. The interview process facilitates hard conversations focusing on a potential team member's sexual brokenness, including any pornography addiction, past sexual abuse, and commitment level.

- Sexual brokenness. Due to the nature of this kind of work, the graphic images that team members will be exposed to online, and the level of trauma they'll encounter, you want to make sure your team is spiritually and emotionally strong, walking in freedom in their own lives before engaging in this kind of direct ministry. Additionally, we recommend that all individuals be pornography-free for at least eighteen months to two years before joining the team.

- Past sexual abuse. Many people desire to help those who have been exploited because they too have had a background of sexual abuse and can personally identify with exploited individuals. This "pay it forward" attitude is wonderful! But as a leader, make sure to discuss this background with applicants and assess that they have experienced distinct levels of healing and breakthrough in their own lives before they accept the responsibility of ministering to others. We recommend any survivors of trafficking who join the team go through at least two years of therapy first and see a therapist currently, to be able to process the way being involved in outreach affects them.

- Commitment level. Discuss the necessary level of commitment to the team and to the exploited individuals they will befriend. Gauging the commitment level of each prospective member is a huge responsibility and essential for building a solid team. If someone has four children and a full-time job, how much time can she or he practically give to a weekly meeting with the team, a weekly online outreach, and the multiple meetings that will follow? People often overcommit themselves on the front end with little idea of the actual investment. Helping them understand the significant time commitment and setting realistic expectations are central to getting mutual buy-in from all team members.

Step 4: Initial training. After acceptance, initiate a training process in which you lay out all of the team's functions, best practices, rules, commitments, and values. Trainings should also include trauma-informed care and survivor-led input wherever possible. (For more information on connecting with trained-survivors who could assist with your training, see www.nationalsurvivornetwork.org or GEM's Survivor Leader Institute http://www.gems-girls.org.)

We highly recommend you connect with survivor-leaders in your community and beyond (especially if you don't have any survivors on your team) for advice and input on your outreach strategies. As a starting point, see www.nationalsurvivornetwork.org or www.rebeccabender.org.

PART 2:
Being Prepared: Researching an Exit Plan

Before your team begins outreach, it is imperative that you make the necessary connections and contacts for resources and programs so that you are prepared when an individual expresses their desire to leave the sex industry.

In your city or area, there will likely be many local services or programs that you will need to research and personally connect with to develop an exit strategy and offer options for the individuals you're reaching. We also highly recommend having a small budget already in place (from your organization, church, or team members). You also want to brainstorm fundraising ideas for a budget that you can draw from once you've started. For example, the individuals may be ready to enter a long-term program immediately, but need a temporary shelter while they apply for the program (the intake process for a safe house can take a few days). Or imagine you meet an underage exploited individual. Then you will need to involve law enforcement immediately. In this situation, already having an established contact in the police force will be important.

As a starting point, call the National Trafficking Hotline Number (+1-888-373-7888) to ask for all of the contacts and resources in their database for your city. Connect with (in person or over the phone) other anti-trafficking organizations or groups in your city to find out what is already being done and where you could assist each other.

Then, as an intervention team, create a form or spreadsheet, using the list on page 105, including the contact name, number, website, and brief details.

During outreach, don't make grandiose promises of restoration and provision on the front end. You might not be able to follow through, and you don't want to promise what you can't guarantee. However, you can assure individuals that if they're ready to exit, you can definitely assist them with this process.

As you build a relationship with the individual, try to help her identify the factors keeping her in exploitation and, as a tri-team, have a potential exit action plan ready for her, all the while supporting her in her own dreams and choices towards freedom.

Then what might be next? Leaving her pimp and entering a shelter? Drug rehab? A long-term residential safe house? A job? Transitional

Intervention in Community

103

living? A sponsored internship? College? GED? Job Core? Connect the exploited individual with as many life-lines and supportive services as possible. Sometimes you will be making calls on their behalf, but wherever you can, sit with them and gently coach them through making the calls themselves. This empowers them and enables them to have a greater sense of ownership over these decisions. Often programs will need to speak with the individual directly.

If they feel ready to apply to a long-term safe house program, we recommend they ideally move at least two hours away from the primary city of their exploitation, and if possible out of state. This reduces risk of local triggers and compromised safety.

Sometimes the National Trafficking Hotline Number or local law enforcement/orgs/churches may be able to help with hotel or travel vouchers for their travel expenses to the program. A discreet (i.e. no names/pictures of victims) online fundraising account could also help with emergency provision.

Our encounters with exploited individuals are sometimes one-off meetings, or at times the relationship builds for a few months but then is cut off if they distance themselves or leave the area. Sometimes, however, we will walk with these individuals for years, seeing amazing breakthroughs and witnessing their restoration process, even attending their weddings and throwing their baby showers! However long or short the length of the path we walk alongside them, we can be confident that God brought us together with them at that time for a purpose, whether it was for one hour or a lifetime.

Exit Plan Contacts List

As an Intervention Team, create a form or spreadsheet using this list (we recommend researching a "Top 5" in each category), including the contact name, number, website, and brief details.

Begin by listing the following:
- Category
- Name
- Number
- Address
- Website
- Details and contact

Make a list of the Top 5 contacts for all of the following:
- Other anti-trafficking organizations/groups in city/area
- Local human trafficking FBI contact
- Local temporary/crisis shelters
- Local domestic violence shelters
- Local temporary detox centers
- Local shelters/safe homes for men
- Non-local safe homes for battered men
- Local long-term programs/safe homes
- Local affordable housing contacts
- Local and non-local transitional living homes
- Local job-assistance centers
- Non-local long-term program/safe homes
- Job Core
- Survivor networks
- Bills assistance contacts
- Businesses/jobs that are hiring
- Recommended local churches/ministries
- Salvation Army
- Food banks
- Clothes banks
- Social services
- Local mental health facilities
- Transportation options/contacts with discounts
- Other key contacts

Intervention in Community

PART 3:
Imperative Security Measures

When meeting with exploited individuals, we must take security very seriously. These victims are often under the control or influence of men or women that could perceive you and your ministry as a legitimate threat. It is imperative that we seek to prevent putting ourselves into dangerous situations. At the same time, Scripture tells us the Holy Spirit is within us, providing discernment. We are partnering with the Lord to make intercession on behalf of His creation and contend for their freedom. We must be cautious and use discernment but not walk in fear.

Security begins with awareness—a necessity in our outreach. A proper awareness of your surroundings is essential to understanding your need of readiness and the correct level of response. To be unaware leaves us feeling helpless, shocked, and unprepared. Below, we've detailed specific security measures for specific types of outreach and intervention and responsibilities of each team member during an intervention.

Security measures for texting outreach and one-on-one meetings:
Avoid any language in texting that may make her suspicious you're a different pimp trying to recruit her to join your group of girls or escorting agency.

Also, be cognizant of the fact that she may be trying to recruit you. Pimps often use their girls to recruit other girls into prostitution. Be alert to her language and anything that sounds like recruitment. Finally, be aware that you could potentially be texting her pimp who might have control of her phone. When setting up an initial meeting, you must speak on the phone with the girl before agreeing to meet with her to ensure you're speaking with her and not a pimp. A phone conversation can also be more personal than texting and can help assure her of your good intentions.

The initial meeting requires the greatest level of security and caution. Once an initial meeting is scheduled, contact the team leader to assemble a tri-team. You'll meet together 45 minutes before the meeting to be briefed on the situation, share a photo of the girl's face with the tri-team, to pray. The team at the first meeting will consist of two women and a security detail—a male who will follow at a distance during the initial meeting. He is there to be an extra set of eyes and an emergency support if something should happen.

Intervention Manual

Security measures for street outreach: In street outreach, being aware of your surroundings is vital. Things change quickly, and people can approach out of nowhere. If you're approached by a volatile person—a drug addict, a pimp, or a passerby—first try to de-escalate the situation. Second, pull the volatile individual aside from where ministry is happening. And third, listen to this person to discern if this is spiritual or simply a distraction. Determine if you're able to talk to them and calm them down, or if you need to simply walk away.

Security measures for pickups and drop-offs: Even though we try to meet victims at public fast food places when possible, sometimes the women don't have a car. In those cases, we ask her (over the phone) to walk to the nearest gas station or an easy-to-find spot nearby (not directly outside the house where she's staying). The security detail should follow in a car behind you. Drop-off happens the same way. Remember to be as aware when you drop her off as you were when you picked her up. Keep watch behind you to make sure no one is following you.

Team Member Roles in Security Measures

Security Detail Role:

In case of an emergency, the security detail will:

- First, call 911.

- Then, call the team leader.

The individual you're meeting with should ideally never see the security detail (on individual meetings, this does not refer to street outreach). Seeing him could hinder any trust building and would probably make her feel unsafe. She could think you're trying to recruit her or that you are a cop.

Below, we've listed the different levels of danger/awareness that the security detail must always be alert to, including the zones and the specific zone the team is operating in throughout the meeting. Teams should always be in Yellow zone but be prepared for Orange at any time.

Levels of Awareness

WHITE:
unaware and thus unprepared

- Obvious lack of concern regarding surroundings
- Inability to respond to threat
- "Head down," not paying attention
- Not showing an in-charge, assertive posture
- Easy prey to anyone wanting to take advantage of weakness or distraction

YELLOW:
a relaxed but alert state of awareness.

- Not in a place where there is an observed threat.
- Watching for what happens or may happen.
- Always watchful for possible danger.
- Alert and thus able to act.
- Posture is head up, scanning the area with a relaxed and in-charge demeanor.

ORANGE:
a specific alert.

- Sense of abnormality is elevated.
- A specific person, car, or situation is observed.
- Mental trigger is set and must remain there until the elevated level is decreased or lifted
- This is not the appropriate level to take action. A response may be premature, but continued heightened awareness is imperative.

RED:
time to take action.

- Your situation is dangerous and requires action.
- Action must happen now.
- A mental trigger has been activated (Examples: the car next to you in traffic has swerved and you must get out of the way; the person you noticed staring at you is out of his chair and quickly closing distance on you.)

Secondary Team Member Role:

The secondary role on the tri-team should be in discreet text communication with the security detail, providing updates but not texting constantly, which might make you appear to be uninterested or rude. If the girl you're meeting with begins to express concerns that her pimp won't be happy she is meeting with you or other warning signs, the secondary team member texts the security detail to brief him that there is a very controlling pimp nearby and to be on guard. Give physical descriptions as you have them. Keep the security detail updated as much you can and listen carefully for pertinent details describing or giving clues to someone's abuse and the level of threat.

Follow-Up Meetings and Exit Plan

After the initial meeting, you should be able to assess the level of threat for future meetings. Again, at the initial meeting you will always have a security detail. For any follow-up meetings, your team should evaluate if a security detail is necessary.

As we emphasized earlier, having a clear exit plan in place for those you minister to is integral to successfully serving them in ways that empower independence instead of creating dependence on you. Make this plan together in your group. Remember that setting clear boundaries on what you're able and willing to do in intervention and what you are not able and are not willing to do is vital. Knowing those boundaries before you start will make adhering to them much easier than if you try to set them as you go.

Meeting Dos and Don'ts to Remember:

Dos	Don'ts
<ul><li>Do remember you can say "no" to any request you aren't comfortable with. For example, if they want you to come inside their house and meet their friends, it's okay to tell them you aren't comfortable with this idea! It's good policy to avoid unknown environments where possible.</li><li>Keep the security detail informed and updated via text.</li><li>Do report all meetings, both before and after the interaction. (See Appendix F for an example of a meeting form.)</li><li>Keep your eyes open at all times and be aware of your surroundings.</li></ul>	<ul><li>Don't leave valuables like your purse, money, or credit cards unattended.</li><li>Don't take pictures with the exploited individual or leave behind anything that she could use to tie back to your identity or put you at risk.</li><li>If a location seems unsafe or she wants to be dropped off at an unknown house, do use caution and drop her off down the street (at a nearby gas station or a store) and let her walk home. Don't pull up in front of the house and don't linger there while you're praying for her.</li></ul>

PART 4:
Sexual Integrity

Part of leading and being part of an intervention team is ensuring that team members are pursuing lifestyles that reflect the same message your team is sending to the exploited. Before we trumpet the message of God's restoration and healing of another's sexuality, we must be deeply connected to the value that God places on our own bodies and His desire for our personal healing and radical integrity in this area. Paul writes to the church of Ephesus:

> "But among you there must not be even a hint of sexual immorality, or of any kind of impurity, or of greed, because these are improper for God's holy people ... For you were once darkness, but now you are light in the Lord. Live as children of light (for the fruit of the light consists in all goodness, righteousness and truth) and find out what pleases the Lord. Have nothing to do with the fruitless deeds of darkness, but rather expose them."
>
> **Eph. 5:3, 8-11**

At the heart of abolition is the belief that every human being is of great worth. God made mankind in His own image (Gen. 1:27). He designed human sexuality to be a sacred expression of a holy, permanent and exclusive covenant within marriage, illustrating the intended depth of union between Jesus and His Bride, the Church (Eph. 5:32).

On every possible level, prostitution undermines God's design for the sexual union, reducing sexuality to an exploitative business transaction. Our passion for ending sexual exploitation for another human must stem from our personal zeal for God's intentions regarding our own sexuality. To truly understand His emotions surrounding this devastating counterfeit expression of sexuality, we urgently need a profound revelation showing us the power and beauty of sexual integrity, whatever our marital status.

In His Sermon on the Mount, Jesus demonstrates His passion to see His people violently break any ties with sexual dehumanization—calling them to a higher standard of integrity:

You have heard that it was said, "You shall not commit adultery," but I say to you that everyone who looks at a woman with lust for her has already committed adultery with her in his heart. If your right eye makes you stumble, tear it out and throw it from you ... (Matt. 5:27-28).

Intervention in Community

In this ministry to the sexually exploited, we are directly confronting the spirit of sexual immorality. By remaining committed to reaching for wholehearted sexual integrity, we

- gain authority in this area through prayer.

- know that the enemy has no territory or grounds for accusation.

- are victorious in the battle of temptation and will not stumble into sexual sin.

As a statement of agreement with these values, we ask that every team member sign a Sexual Integrity Commitment Form, which outlines outward, practical expressions of our inward commitment and consecration. (See Appendix C for an example of a Sexual Integrity Commitment Form you can use or adapt for your ministry.)

Personal sanctification is a lifelong process. But daily reaching for sexual integrity in our hearts, minds, and bodies must be a core lifestyle choice for every believer, especially those called to fight sexual exploitation. We are called to be conformed into the likeness of Christ and to be holy as He is holy. God is a good, kind, and generous Father. He can supply the grace and power to walk in the beauty of His holiness that He desires for His children. All conscious sin in your hearts should be addressed, prayed through and fought against (greed, envy, pride, etc.).

Can I Stay Pure Doing this Outreach?

People interested in starting a ministry to sexually exploited victims often ask us about the effects of entering and being exposed to such intense and sexually charged environments. Some people refrain from being involved in this kind of ministry out of fear of compromising their holiness/integrity.

Though their questions are valid, often those questions are based in fear and religiosity more than in wisdom and a willingness to obey and follow Christ's example.

Look at the examples Jesus gave us in His ministry:

- The Son of God was without sin. He was not afraid of entering environments and situations that would normally be considered defiling for a Jewish rabbi. He knew the Father had sent Him to bring the Kingdom of light and love to those places and people. Jesus brought transformation to environments and individuals, and that is the vision He sets before us—to go without fear and bring light into the darkness.

- In Section 1, we detailed why Jesus took His disciples to Caesarea Philippi (Matthew 16). The region was known as the epicenter of Greek idol worship where immorality (such as temple prostitution and child sacrifice) took place. Built into the huge surrounding rock were countless shrines to the half-man/half-goat god Pan and many other overtly phallic and sexual idols. There, Jesus declared, "On this rock (in dark, perverted places like this), I will build My church and the gates of Hades shall not prevail." Jesus' desire for His Church is to invade the darkest places, build an altar to *Yahweh*, and bring transformation and healing.

- Jesus ate with sinners who became radical disciples and friends of God (Zacchaeus in Luke 19:1-10; Matthew in Matthew 9:9-13).

- In the parable of the Good Samaritan (Luke 10:25), the priest and Levite may well have avoided helping the attacked man covered in blood for fear of defilement according to the law. But Jesus explained that He desires for us to love our neighbor by going to them in their bloody, dirty, and even naked state; bringing them to a safe place; paying for their expenses; practically helping them; and then returning to them. This is what true compassion and loving our neighbor looks like in Jesus' eyes.

Throughout the gospels, Jesus goes to the sick to make them well and to the place of death to bring life. He goes to the darkness to bring light and to the broken to mend. Transformation takes place wherever He goes. And He calls His bride to partner with Him in this mission.

In his gospel account, Mark insightfully defines defilement:

"Nothing outside a person can defile them by going *into* them. Rather, it is what comes *out of* a person that defiles them" (Mark 7:15, italics added).

From this we understand that going into a strip club to minister to exploited women is not defiling! Praying for a half-naked person on the street does not defile us. Neither does seeing an image of a scantily clad woman on the internet. These individuals are men and women bearing the image of God. They have an eternal soul and are worth the spilled blood of Jesus. They have extreme value in His eyes, and His heart burns with love for them.

We are defiled on the inside (in our attitudes, thoughts, and motivations and when we make agreement with the enemy's ideas rather than Jesus')—not by the things we see and hear on the outside (environment, people, and images). We do recognize that we need to use wisdom and we don't place male team members (especially those who've battled with pornography in the past) in sexually charged environments.

Redeeming Our Scars

In this ministry, we will encounter scenes that deeply disturb us. We can pray for such images to be removed from our minds—or we can choose to ask God to redeem them.

We will be impacted and scarred by what we see, but may they be holy scars like the scars Jesus still bears on His own body—the scars that continue to fuel our urgency to reach exploited men and women in captivity. May the scars remind us of this injustice and stir us into action again and again.

We will not forget the photo on the website of the frightened girl, wearing red lingerie and handcuffs and cowering in the corner with despair in her eyes. We will not forget the almost naked boy on the streets with blisters and scabs who wept as we hugged him and told him he was loved. We will not forget the empty expression on the face of a topless Brazilian girl who was made to crawl like a cat on a stage before men in a strip club. We will not forget the girl in the yellow summer dress on a Backpage ad that said she was 18 but an appearance indicating she was closer to 15. Jesus has not forgotten them, and neither will we.

> *"God asks His people, 'Who will go?' He invites us to go to the places where He isn't known to make Him known."*

When we are in the darkest environments, sharing His love with the most broken individuals, we often feel His light within us blaze the brightest and His compassion flow through us the strongest. When we take His presence to places that many might fear to go, we are entering a divine partnership. God asks His people, "Who will go?" He invites us to go to the places where He isn't known to make Him known. It is a holy and precious invitation to deeper intimacy with Jesus because when we go, we will find Him already there.

PART 5:
Men in Outreach

In the crisis of modern-day slavery, men have been the primary abusers, traffickers, and johns. Their complicity in this crime has been widespread and often shocking. However, men can play a critical role in the solution to this injustice. We welcome whole, healthy men who walk in the fear of the Lord to step into roles of support, encouragement, and fathering throughout the outreach community and to minister to the exploited men and women we serve.

At Exodus Cry, we're often asked if men should be involved in outreach. The answer is simply, "yes." Because men are so often the perpetrators in this injustice, the enemy would like us to believe that men are disqualified, shamed, and can only serve as part of the problem. In reality, strong, committed men are instrumental in this fight and integral to its success.

In Christ, men can be an essential part of the restoration process, helping to liberate hearts and offering a voice of compassion. For those exploited individuals who are in the process of healing, godly males can provide them an opportunity to develop positive relationships with men. Men make up half the population, so it would be impossible for anyone who has suffered sexual abuse at the hands of men to go through life post-exploitation and never interact with men. Completely sheltering someone from society is not true restoration.

Instead, men must model to women a healthy, loving, honoring, and respectful relationship between men and women—beginning in the outreach context at a safe relational distance and continuing throughout the restoration process in the context of a family. Godly men can serve as a positive example by speaking a blessing and life over a woman's identity, honoring her, and treating her with dignity and respect—in some cases, the first time she has ever been treated that way by a man. Affirmations like these can draw exploited women and children out of shame and into healing.

Women on the streets are also used to men looking at them with either lust or disgust. When a godly man looks into an exploited woman's eyes with kindness, respect, and dignity, he is being the eyes of Jesus to her in that moment, and the impact is often profound. The way male team members treat and serve the female team members as their sisters in Christ is also a powerful witness.

In the Footsteps of Jesus

Throughout Scripture, Jesus gives us a powerful picture of how men are to walk compassionately in this world. His life is a picture of a man who met with the hurting and sexually broken. Instead of staying sheltered behind church walls, moved by compassion Jesus actively reached out to exploited persons, and great wonders followed.

Jesus displayed a fellowship with the suffering and knew every facet of the human experience so that He could feel the same pain. If an eternal Holy God can meet people in their greatest despair, then why wouldn't we follow this example? The gospel of Luke tells us that the same power, the same love, and the same man lives in us.

In Luke 4, Jesus quotes Isaiah 61 saying, "The Spirit of the Lord is upon Me, because He has anointed Me to preach the gospel to the poor; He has sent Me to heal the brokenhearted, to proclaim liberty to the captives and recovery of sight to the blind, to set at liberty those who are oppressed; to proclaim the acceptable year of the Lord" (Luke 4:18-19, ERV).

Putting On the Heart and Mind of Christ

The most practical way that men can follow in Jesus' footsteps and be a presence for healing is to cultivate pure hearts and minds.

Men so often think that they are just slaves to lust, unable to overcome the evil that pervades our culture. But Scripture tells us that we have been set free from sin and are slaves to righteousness (Rom. 6:18). When we pursue that righteousness, we begin to take on the mind of Christ and begin seeing women as our sisters and daughters, not as a commodity to be consumed. There is nothing sexy about sexual exploitation.

A male team member who once struggled with pornography addiction in his past said, "I used to be part of the problem, but now I can help be part of the solution."

Serving in this kind of ministry will require a great deal of honesty and accountability. The dialogue begins with a conversation about our own hearts. We must talk about sexual integrity, own our shortcomings, and find hope and resolve from the example of Jesus and the shared accountability of our brothers.

If your heart is pure, you are not defiled when you enter these dark places and witness the suffering and exploitation. Exploited men and women are not going to taint you. Those kinds of pious thoughts tend to bolster our excuses to stay on the sidelines and essentially relegate us to Pharisees who look good on the outside but whose hearts are unclean. If we're in Christ, then we can walk out of a red-light district as pure and as clean as when we walked in.

If you're personally struggling with pornography or sexual immorality, then you're not ready to be in this kind of ministry. If you're not walking in freedom, then you cannot adequately participate in someone else's path to freedom. We need discernment about entering into this kind of ministry and the sexually charged environments we'll encounter. Simply put, if men are struggling with pornography and sexual immorality, then they aren't the best witnesses in these places.

But to think that all men are this way and can never overcome these things is a lie. Think about it: Your sexual integrity can be the crucial characteristic of humanity that sets the captives free! Putting on the mind of Christ is not just some Christian principle. It could make the difference between someone's freedom or enslavement.

All over the earth, men and women are longing for a word of life, a spark of hope, and a person of compassion and kindness to come and illuminate the darkness of their exploitation. The harvest is plentiful, but the laborers are few. We need an army of men and women walking boldly—with pure hearts and intentions—into the white harvest of the red-light districts, back alley brothels, and streets with the message of hope through eternal life.

A few practical things for male team members to remember:

- Your presence on outreaches enables the female team members to minister in safety. Without men, many forms of outreach would not (and should not) happen. Therefore, get well trained in security and be attentive at all times.

- Smile and look friendly! Being a security detail does not mean you need to look intimidating. However, allow the female team members to initiate conversation with the women where possible and wait for them to introduce you as a safe person and friend.

- Look into the eyes of the women on the streets: the windows to their humanity. Don't look at her body parts, but keep your eyes respectfully on her face at all times.

- Never touch a woman on the streets without permission.

- By being involved in this work, you are a rare breed and setting a new culture for men.

Exodus Cry Team Testimony: Marshall

Every outreach I go on, my heart comes more alive for the men and women I meet.

Since joining the intervention team with Exodus Cry, my eyes have been opened in new ways to the injustice that's happening locally and worldwide. Before joining the team, I thought that sex trafficking mainly occurred in poverty-stricken areas of other countries, and that prostitution was only something happening in major U.S. cities. I was wrong. Both are happening daily—right here in my own town, a few miles away from my front door step.

I joined the outreach team mainly to serve as security and support for the girls on the team, but God had more in store for me. Every outreach I go on, my heart comes more alive for the men and women I meet. I have a real desire for them to know the Father's love. The face-to-face conversations with these men and women awaken my heart to truly fight for them. When I meet a prostituted individual on the street, I see a broken and hurting child longing for love. These are my brothers and sisters. I truly believe God loves each one of them just as much as He loves me, and He desires that they come to know Him as a Father!

It's now my heart's desire and mission to see freedom come into the life of every person I meet on the streets. God has been faithful to take my weak prayers and attempts to love and use them for good. It's His power and love alone that heals and brings true freedom. I often wonder if my own heart is awakening with compassion and love for these individuals, how much more does God (the one who knit each one of us together in our mother's womb) desire for them to know Him as Father! I count it all joy to serve on this team.

TESTIMONY ✎
Breakthrough by Prayer: Gabriella's Story

I (Helen) and another intervention volunteer established a connection with Gabriella after she responded to a texting outreach. We met at a nearby fast food restaurant, and there we heard her story and of her desire to leave "the life." She had run away from home as a teenager and, as commonly happens, exploitation soon followed.

Gabriella felt that getting a job would be her only way out. We arranged to meet her again to help her write her first job resumé. Over the next two months, we would meet Gabriella twice a week to help her apply for jobs, both online and in person. We encouraged her to consider long-term safe programs and talked her through what that would entail. She insisted she wasn't ready for this yet, so we respected her choice. In the midst of providing the practical support of rides and applications, our time together intertwined with building trust and friendship. As a result of her vulnerability, Gabriella ended up being prostituted on the streets of various cities all over the United States.

We had many opportunities to pray with Gabriella and empower her with the truth of how God sees her. I asked the Lord for a scripture to personally pray over her, as a weapon of warfare. He gave me Hosea 11, which speaks of His "cords of human kindness." I felt that every act of love offered in His name became a cord, drawing Gabriella towards Jesus.

Gabriella adored the Bible and journal we gave her in the Hope Bag. She wrote out scripture quotes into the journal we gave her. Her favorite verse was Jeremiah 1:5: "Before I formed you in the womb I knew you, before you were born I set you apart; I appointed you as a prophet to the nations."

Gabriella's life was quite dysfunctional and chaotic at this stage. She moved from motel to motel with her "boyfriend," who took her earnings from exploitation to support his destructive lifestyle habits. We were aware that even if she obtained a new job, she would still be living with her boyfriend, who would likely take her money and demand that she make more. We began to wonder if the reason the Lord hadn't opened any doors for jobs was because He wanted Gabriella out of Kansas City.

Around this time, my ministry partner and I met up solely to intercede for Gabriella. We strongly felt she was on the cusp of a breakthrough.

Intervention in Community

We completely surrendered our own human solutions in exchange for God's answer. After praying, we both felt that something had shifted. We had great faith that something was about to change for the better!

The very next morning Gabriella texted to tell me that her father had contacted her the night before, inviting her to permanently move back in with him and her family who lived out of state. She had not seen them in many years. In the time since she had run away as a teenager, her parents had kept in touch with her, but had never once asked her to move back in with them. It was as though her father had a wake-up call—his daughter was in a dangerous situation, and she needed to get home.

Gabriella couldn't contain her excitement: "My dad wants me home! They're giving me a second chance! They're paying for my ticket, and I'm leaving this weekend in time for Thanksgiving!" We had one last meet-up before she left. We treated her to a professional makeover and bought her a new pair of shoes to symbolize the new identity and season she was entering into. In exchange, Gabriella gave us the old, silver high heels that she had worn during her life of exploitation. Upon arriving at her parents' home, she got a job immediately. She is with them to this day, rebuilding her life.

A few days after Gabriella left, I re-read the scripture the Lord had led me to pray over her before we first met. The last verse said: "'And I will settle them in their homes,' declares the Lord" (Hosea 11:11). I saw that the Lord had been preparing a plan all along and that His ways were higher than ours. His desire for Gabriella was reconciliation and redemption—to leave Kansas City (and her boyfriend) and be united again with her family.

Through this journey, I realized how vital it is that we minister to these girls from the place of prayer, connected to the Lord's heart and plans, and not merely based on human logic which offers temporary solutions. The ultimate breakthrough comes from God's intervention. We must commit to intercede for His heavenly solutions to be released in the lives of these precious girls who long to exit a life of sexual exploitation for good.

SECTION 5:
Resources

PART 1

126

Working with Law Enforcement

PART 2

128

Trauma and Self-Care

PART 3

140

Recommended Reading

PART 4

146

The Current Landscape of Exploitation

PART 5

152

Legal Approaches to Prostitution Legalization Worldwide

PART 1:
Working with Law Enforcement

To reach the thousands of trafficking victims in the United States annually, law enforcement, service providers, and the local community must be knowledgeable about human trafficking, its existence, victim assistance, how to bring traffickers to justice—and what it looks like to collaborate to accomplish these goals.

When working together, law enforcement and service providers can educate and teach each other about human trafficking and their respective roles and efforts. Law enforcement can learn about human trafficking issues from service providers and then train their fellow officers. In turn, service providers can learn from law enforcement about local efforts, including what police require from a trafficking victim (a statement, an affidavit, etc.) to start an investigation and prosecution.

Partnering can also save each other time. For example, a trafficking victim may need several weeks or even months to reveal the complexities of her situation. Often local law enforcement doesn't have the time or manpower to gain a victim's trust and discover the truth about the trafficking situation. When that happens, law officers can enlist the assistance of service providers who can work with the victim to make a statement or prepare her to be a better witness. Service providers can also assist a victim with time-consuming tasks such as finding housing, obtaining health care, accessing mental health services, and applying for federal and state benefits—giving law enforcement time to focus on the prosecution of the case.

Before a trafficking victim needs assistance from your group, make it a priority to develop relationships with local law enforcement and other service providers. Both law enforcement agencies and service providers must see and respect each other as organizations and partners in combating human trafficking. No one agency can efficiently or effectively fight the great atrocity of human trafficking alone.

Intervention Manual

Tips for building relationships with law enforcement:

- Contact the human trafficking task force in your city and arrange to meet with an agent on the task force or vice squad.

- Alternatively, you could invite a representative to come and speak to your team or group.

- Identify and learn about local victim care services in your community.

- Identify practical ways you can serve each other and work together to locate victims of commercial sexual exploitation and offer assistance.

- Research and know the action steps to take if an exploited woman chooses to prosecute and press charges against her pimp/trafficker.

- If you ever meet an individual who tells you she is being trafficked (or implies that force, fraud, or coercion is currently being used to keep them in prostitution against their will), inform law enforcement immediately!

- If you ever meet an underage individual on the streets or online being commercially sexually exploited, immediately notify and involve law enforcement (by calling 911), regardless of whether or not the victim wants this help.

- For additional training on building relationship, with law enforcement, see www.rebeccabender.org. Under "shop" you will find these resources.

PART 2:
Trauma and Self-Care

Keeping Our Hearts Centered

"My child, give attention to my words; incline your ear to my sayings. Do not let them depart from your eyes; keep them in the midst of your heart; For they are life to those who find them, and health to all their flesh. Keep your heart with all diligence, for out of it springs the issues of life. Put away from you a deceitful mouth, and put perverse lips far from you" (Prov. 4:10-14).

Keeping our hearts centered is a matter of our focus on and obedience to the Word of God. In the midst of the daily labor and concerns of life, Jesus specifies the one essential thing we need to put into practice—sitting at His feet and hearing His words. We do not live by bread alone, but by every word from the Lord. His speech is full of the grace, truth, and life that are absolutely necessary for our hearts. Remember His words to Martha, the sister of Mary:

"Martha, Martha, you are worried and troubled about many things. But one thing is needed, and Mary has chosen that good part, which will not be taken away from her" (Luke 10:41),

The Impact of Emotional Pain

As you begin to work with exploited individuals, listening to their stories and attending to their needs, the importance of being sensitive to and responding to your own emotional pain will increase. Pain inevitably has an effect upon us all. No one is immune to it; however, our responses to pain can vary. Our individual responses will determine how pain shapes and affects us. Consider these possible responses to pain:

- Pain can become all-consuming. When we allow pain to take over, we experience a significant decrease (if not altogether absence) in our regular meditation on the promises of God. We can only continue on this route for so long before being utterly consumed with pain—traumatized, disillusioned, confused, despairing, bitter, and burnt out. If we let this happen, the question remains: *How can our loss of hope help restore the hopeless?*

- Pain can cause us to disassociate and begin to lose much of our "present." We begin losing self-awareness and attention to the world around us. At the height of this response, we begin to experience the same symptoms the women we're working to free are experiencing. The line becomes blurred between our sense of a healthy self and the self we're attempting to restore in someone else. Their crisis of faith and crisis of identity become ours. The question becomes: *How does our disconnectedness and isolation help to reintegrate others in need of loving community?*

- Pain can numb us, making us jaded and calloused with an internal attitude of "seen that, done that." The real-life stories of women become depersonalized to us. When this happens, eventually, we feel nothing. We consider ourselves experts on pain and competent to handle anything because we think we're above it. Full of prideful self-reliance, void of true compassion and comfort, we don't give God the room to increase our capacity, and instead become greatly diminished. When this happens, the questions become: *How can the loss of our hearts help restore the hearts of others? How can our inability to give and receive love help to create this capacity in others?*

The answer to all of these questions is, "We can't." We can't respond to pain in our own strength. We must keep our hearts centered. Because we are participants in the power of His resurrection, we can confidently say "yes" to feeling what God feels and allow pain to touch us. We can fellowship in His way of suffering, empowered by the truth that the same Spirit who raised Christ from the dead lives in us. The resurrection offers a safe context for fellowshipping in the long-suffering character of God. Only through Him is the feeling of pain given a transcendent hope.

When it all becomes too much to bear, we need a haven. It is right and good to retreat into the comfort and security of the Lord's embrace, knowing that He continues to carry those women He has shared with you. He is both your Shepherd and hers. There is need for transcendence. Establish a place (both physical and in your imagination) where you can spend private time with God. Seek safe environments with friends and family who can help to nurture you.

We can be assured through the shared pain that He is working in us what the apostle Paul calls "an eternal weight of glory," using every opportunity to conform us to His image.

"Therefore we do not lose heart. Even though our outward man is perishing, yet the inward man is being renewed day by day. For our light affliction, which is but for a moment, is working for us a far more exceeding and eternal weight of glory, while we do not look at the things which are seen, but at the things which are not seen. For the things which are seen are temporary, but the things which are not seen are eternal" (2 Cor. 4:16-18 NKJV).

Clinical Terminology: Trauma[1]

Putting words to what you or a woman you're helping is experiencing can be vital to understanding and then identifying the effective treatment or approach for it. Below, we've listed several terms associated with trauma you can familiarize yourself with:

Vicarious trauma: negative changes that can take place in trauma workers across time.

According to the American Counseling Association, vicarious trauma is the emotional residue of exposure that counselors have from working with people as they listen to their trauma stories and become witnesses to the pain, fear, and terror that trauma survivors have endured. The loss of innocence that some helpers experience as their worldviews shift may induce grief, which is another dimension of vicarious trauma.

Countertransference: the therapist's responses to a single client, whether trauma is involved or not.

Countertransference can serve as an effective tool in discerning the psychological state of the individual. Example: An exploitation victim presents herself as calm and collected, yet the helper feels a rise of anxiety and tension in her chest with a sense that the victim could lunge at her any second. The helper is experiencing underlying anger and fear.

Still, it's important to stay aware of your emotions and maintain a sense of "separateness," while remaining attuned to the emotions of the victim. Be aware of close resemblances in personal family dynamics, culture of origin, or traumatic experiences, and be careful not to respond out of unresolved personal issues. Don't assume that the client wants the same type of response you would want.

> *"It's important to stay aware of your emotions and maintain a sense of 'separateness,' while remaining attuned to the emotions of the victim."*

Stay attuned to her, asking the Holy Spirit to contain your needs for the moment and to give you wisdom into the heart of this woman. Afterwards, be sure to address your feelings and needs with a trusted counselor, colleague, mentor, friend, or family member.

Empathetic attunement: the capacity to resonate efficiently and accurately to another's state of being; to match self/other understanding; to have knowledge of the internal psychological ego states of another who has suffered a trauma; and to understand the unique internal working model of their trauma experience.

Burnout: the gap between what the helper expects herself to accomplish and the reality of what she is actually able to accomplish.

Contagion: an unconscious exchange of traumatic material (thoughts, feelings, and imagery).

Compassion fatigue: parallel trauma symptoms that helpers may develop in working with traumatized victims.

Wilder's Guidelines for Trauma Teams[2]

Learn to feel helpless: You can't witness God's great works without feeling helpless. Nor can you hear about evil without feeling helpless.

Come to terms with evil: Unless we understand our own evil temptations enough to feel the pull of evil, we will be of little help in understanding the struggles of others when we form loving family bonds with them. If we cannot deal effectively with evil, we will be either seduced by it or scared off.

Work one step at a time: Bonding with God advances in stages as we progressively bring Him into one area of our lives and then another and so on. When someone begins to wake from a coma, parts of the mind come out of the coma and are conditioned to believe that they're still in the original disaster. Each piece must learn the good news individually.

Teach through examples: For a long time, the exploited victims you work with will see Jesus as being like us. Through our bonds, others come to be like us. Let's hope we are becoming like the hearts Jesus gave us.

Seek healing: Following Jesus requires truth, power, and relationship. God transforms identities through the bonds we form. Traumas of the past maintain their power in the present only when the trauma is connected to some lie that's still active.

Learn and practice discernment: Discernment is found among the wise, not necessarily in the smart or old.

Pursue personal integrity: Bonding with victims of sexual perversion exposes our every weakness. If we have problems with anger or vengeance, this work has plenty to tempt us. If we struggle with lust, we can face intense sexual feelings. If we suffer from fear, terror can rock us. If we have a need to make things fair, we could be in for a crisis of faith. If we need to be sure about everything, we could be in for confusion. If we are prone to escape into work, this work will consume us. If we want a fight, this one can be almost endless. If we cannot return to joy from anger, fear, shame, disgust, or hopeless despair, we will be down for the count. Satan and our own potential to do evil and call it good will reliably provide their own escapes, elixirs, potions, and quick pressure releases.

Get familiar with your own temptations and vices. On a hard day, where do you look for comfort and escape outside of Jesus? It is wise to set personal boundaries such as, "When I've had an intense or challenging day, I will not binge on media/junk food/alcohol/shopping/novels/fill in the blank." Keeping these things associated with positivity, celebration, rest, and fellowship keeps them in their rightful place as servants, not masters. Unchecked vices can lead to addiction and idolatry, and only in Jesus do we find the true comfort, peace, and rest that our souls so desperately need.

Integrity keeps us within our boundaries or limits even as we expand our knowledge base and learn more about our capabilities. Integrity keeps us honest. We must know what we can do and what we cannot.

Prayerfully seek truth: When dealing with people who have practiced deception and have been deceived by others, solid ground can be hard to find. We must seek truth with endurance. We must be prepared to find, hear, and speak truth.

Rest: To maintain our connection to God, we must rest. When we do, we demonstrate our faith, trusting that when we have done our work, God will perfect it. When we rest, God works and fights for us. Resting also involves a certain measure of giving up control.

Find an anchor: Ask at least 10 people to pray for you and have at least three people who will listen to your worst fears and most perverse reactions. Stay close to at least one person who is not afraid to ask you tough questions.

Redeem every bit of history: We need to know and trust that God can and will redeem everything we've been through. God is not done with our history until it becomes the story of how He saved us and made us like His Son. We can return to joy only from the misery we confess. Remember, God is the master of time. He is eternal.

Handle hazardous waste carefully: When you have faced a new horror, tell your support people how it has affected you without sharing the actual story. You want to contain the toxic part but share the burden of your feelings. You need people who believe you when you say you are hurting—someone with the joy to deal with it must do decontamination work. Sometimes we have to apply a little pressure to keep people from bleeding out.

Avoid toxic buildup: Flush your system regularly by praying and singing the Psalms. The words of Scripture can help us return to joy.

Meditate on the law of God: We need this meditation to develop an innate awareness of the difference between good and evil. When we encounter this kind of evil, we cannot understand forgiveness without first understanding His law.

Remember to play: Play together and enjoy the bounty of God's provision and love. Playing helps burn up hazardous waste and makes us glad to be together again. Play builds our joyful identities.

Watch for traumatic bonding: Fears should neither control us nor be dismissed. Attempting to prevent recurrence of an upsetting event often covers a trauma bond. This is particularly likely when the helper is driven to stay involved and cannot pass the problem on to others who will help. By sharing a painful event with someone, we return to joy, and the power of the trauma is broken. Then it's time for rest and fun.

Return to joy: When God has redeemed our hearts, joy is our heart's natural state. When we find ourselves outside of joy, we know we're away from home. When we see others without joy, we need to recognize their need. Remember that the ability to find joy is more important than painful memories, understanding and empathy, our ministry, or even completing the task at hand. Joy is our litmus test as to whether or not we are on track personally in our efforts to fight injustice.

Self-Care

"A rescuer who cannot call for assistance is not much good, nor is a rescuer who becomes disabled in the rescue process."
—E. James Wilde

How can we care for ourselves—mind, bod,y and spirit? In addition to keeping our hearts centered, we can also enlist some disciplines in our daily lives to keep us grounded:

- Choose a Sabbath day and keep it holy. Sabbath is a mindset, as well as an actual day of the week. Allow Jesus to wash your feet on a regular basis. Something about this is an actual qualifier for participation with Him in Kingdom work. It is a check for our heart posture and our awareness of our need for His loving care and washing. Unless you allow Him to minister to you, you can have no part with Him. Remember what Jesus told Peter when He knelt to wash his feet:

    "Peter said to Him, 'You shall never wash my feet!' Jesus answered him, 'If I do not wash you, you have no part with Me.' Simon Peter said to Him, 'Lord, not my feet only, but also my hands and my head!'" (John 13:8-9).

- **Work on keeping your priorities in order.** The church of Ephesus had incredible works, but love for Jesus was always meant to come first. The slip of order was not a casual issue before the Lord. He calls the church to turn back to Him as their source for all life and love. The work itself has potential of becoming an idol. We must be careful to check where our affections are tied.

- **Define the relationship.** Often, girls who have been sexually exploited have grown up in environments with no value for healthy living or mutual relationships. We cannot assume they share our same values and wants for healing. They may not yet. They are often intuition experts and can readily sense that we value their healing, which can be used as leverage to get something out of us: "I'll stay if …" "I'll try if …" "I'll stay out of prostitution as long as …"

When we empower them, we help them assume personal responsibility, just as we own responsibility for our personal self-care and ongoing decisions we make for our health. Communicate clear expectations and define the goal of relationship. Establishing a foundation will uphold you under pressure. If one party has no investment, relationship is easily abandoned, leaving the other party exhausted and disillusioned.

- **Know your limitations.** They reveal our need for God in all relationships and are equalizers for all humans. Know your "hooks" and the patterns that prevent rest. What area of need or who specifically do you find yourself making exceptions for when you have purposed to set boundaries? Is there something you feel responsible for that is not yours? Know your strengths and how they're best used. Sometimes our greatest gifts can be our greatest liabilities when used out of context. (For example, stubbornness gets things done and perseveres through difficulty, but stubbornness can also keep us from letting go of an unhealthy relationship.)

Only Jesus can make these statements:

"No suffering will ever be too much for me bear. I will prove to others that their trauma is never too much for me to hear and feel with them."

"I will always be available to you when you need me."

"I will never leave you."

Self-Care Dos

- Model holistic living and take care of your body. Victims learn to be disconnected from their bodies and have little esteem for the body's value. Show them something different by treating your body well.

- Keep regular doctor visits and be diligent with your physical well-being.

- Consistently go to the dentist and maintain oral care.

- Find ways to relax and relieve tension. Consider massage therapy, chiropractic visits, warm baths, or other means of muscle-tension release and management.

- Pamper yourself periodically with spa days and special treatments.

- Eat three balanced meals daily. Keep well hydrated.

- Determine the number of hours your system requires for proper reset. Set boundaries around your time to meet this goal as consistently as possible.

- Keep a journal, narrating and chronicling your journey and how God and others are walking with you through it.

- Identify and stay involved in things that inspire you and are beautiful to you (fine arts, dance, literature, travel, nature, family, friendships).

- Identify and be intentional to do things that you enjoy or make you laugh (clean comedy movies, friendships, live sports, musicals, animals).

- Create (pottery, gardening, artwork, crafts, writing, refurbishing antiques).

- Demolish (punching bag, kickboxing).

- Keep music in your life. Listen, sing, and worship. Melody goes deeper than words, and ongoing communion with God happens here. Worship can also be a weapon of warfare. When we see the reality of evil, we must grasp the reality of God. Worship aligns our focus, renews our vision, and releases the power and presence of God in the midst of battle.

- Remain close to and engaged with safe people in your life. We must have relationships with those to whom we can confess our deepest struggles and greatest joys.

Cautions—Subtle Yet Deadly Seeds

As you practice self-care, be aware of negative emotions and feelings that can creep in and plant deadly seeds, which will eventually spread and take over your heart, snuffing out your joy. Below are several of the most common feelings plus specific tools for battling these emotions.

Cynicism: nasty speech, distrusting, disparaging, holding a low opinion of humanity, bitterly or sneeringly distrustful, contemptuous, or pessimistic.

Combatting cynicism: Meditate on the return of Jesus, the perfection and unity of His Church, and the establishment of His Kingdom of righteousness and justice on the earth. Read the books of Isaiah, Zechariah, Daniel, and Revelation (accompanied by commentaries).

Despair: to lose, to give up, deep gloom, a state of mind caused by circumstances that seem too much to cope with, disheartenment, total hopelessness.

Combatting despair: Meditate on our coming redemption and focus on the Spirit of all comfort and hope. Read the Psalms, the gospels, and Revelation (accompanied by commentaries). We must intimately know God as the beginning and the end; the One who was, who is, and who is to come.

Fear: a distressing emotion aroused by impending danger, evil, or pain, whether or not the threat is real or imagined; concern or anxiety.

Fighting fear: Meditate on His perfect love that casts out fear.

Bitterness/offense: having a harsh, disagreeably acrid taste; hard to bear; grievous; causing pain; piercing; stinging; characterized by intense antagonism or hostility.

Fighting bitterness: Meditate on the miracle of the cross and resurrection, pointing to His unspeakable mercy and forgiveness, abounding kindness and patience, and selfless love demonstrated for us, which establishes renewed gratitude and awe in our hearts. Sing the hymns of the Psalms (Psalm 103:1-5) and read through Paul's letters (for example, Ephesians 4:31-32) and Revelation (for example, Rev. 15:3) accompanied by commentaries.

Numbness/indifference/depletion of passion: deprived of sensation or the ability to move; incapable of action or feeling emotion; paralyzed; lack of interest or concern; to exhaust the abundance or supply of motivation, purpose, vision. Evil deadens and dulls our spirits; righteousness invigorates and resurrects them.

Easing numbness: Stay close to the fire of God's eyes, meditate on His zeal and His constant intercession for the fullness of our salvation, and explore a study of God's emotions in Scripture. Take whatever emotion you are identifying and consume the Word, searching Scripture and dialoguing with the Lord regarding each one. Empathetic attunement has a real effect on us, which is appropriate and necessary to process both with Jesus and within trusting relationships (outside the context of direct interaction with victims).

Continue to know yourself from God's perspective and insight. We all have unspoken rules governing our emotional lives—shaped by our upbringing, models of communication and emotional processing, and significant life experiences. Is any part of your internal government hindering encounter with God? Is there any static on the line between you and Him, inhibiting His desire to freely give you all of His benefits? Allow His light and His love to permeate you—body, mind, and spirit.

The famous "justice" passage in Isaiah 58 outlines the true fasting that God chooses: loosing the chains of injustice and setting the oppressed free. The glorious promise given to those who do not turn away from their own flesh and blood but instead partner with God's justice is:

"The Lord will guide you always, he will satisfy your needs in a sun-scorched land and will strengthen your frame. You will be like a well-watered garden, like a spring whose waters never fail ... you will be called repairer of broken walls, restorer of streets with dwellings" (Isa. 58:11-12).

The well of the Holy Spirit never runs dry! His love never fails. As you stay connected to the source of all life, may He direct your path, sustain you in this work, continually refresh your weary soul and

Intervention Manual

ever draw your heart deeper into love that truly satisfies, found in the face of Jesus Christ.

The End of the Story

In the midst of such evil and devastating injustice in our world today, we can be full of hope, for He has told us the end of the story and what is to come. The Just King returns to reign. There will be no more pain or sorrow. He will wipe away every tear and put right every wrong.

He wins the battle.

Trafficking will be no more.

But until that day, we will partner with Him on the front line and help bring His light and love to a broken world.

PART 3:
Recommended Reading

Exodus Cry recommends taking the time to prayerfully seek out and research the issue of sex trafficking and prostitution. We believe that prayer is our primary weapon against injustice and issues of sin. Particularly crucial to learn from are historical figures known as intercessory abolitionists (such as Dietrich Bonhoeffer and William Wilberforce) whose works and actions were consistently grounded in a place of prayer.

Begin to familiarize yourself with the issue of sex trafficking nationally and internationally. The following books will serve as useful resources for knowledge and understanding on the injustice of sex trafficking from authors who have a breadth of experience and wisdom. Note that not every author on this list writes from a Christ-centered perspective, but their insights are valuable and worth knowing. Ultimately, the Holy Spirit is our teacher, so we encourage you to intentionally dialogue with the Lord as you read and go at a pace your heart and mind can handle, leaving at the cross any lingering heaviness. Greater understanding on these issues empowers us to pray and to serve with excellence, wisdom, and accuracy.

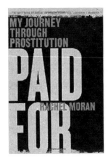

Paid For
My Journey Through Prostitution by Rachel Moran

Moran's enlightening memoir unveils the truthful depravity of prostitution and exposes the many societal myths about the sex trade. Moran eloquently weaves in critical feminist thought and delivers an extremely compelling argument against legalizing prostitution, giving weighty reasoning for why the sex industry must be abolished and the equality (Nordic) model implemented.

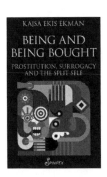

Being And Being Bought:
Prostitution, Surrogacy and the Split Self

Kajsa Ekis Ekman

Swedish activist Ekman brilliantly unpacks the psychological affects of prostitution and the nature of inherent coercion in the commercial sex industry. The second half of this book looks at the issue of surrogacy, but we wholeheartedly recommend this book as one of the clearest written evaluations of CSE in print.

Amazing Grace
Eric Metaxas

Biography of William Wilberforce, abolitionist during the Trans-Atlantic slave trade. Wilberforce is a forerunner for Exodus Cry, walking the ancient path of abolition while upholding morality and deep affection for Jesus. His unrelenting burden for the ending of slavery for more than 40 years makes Wilberforce the "Father of Abolition."

Renting Lacy
Linda Smith

Linda Smith, founder of Shared Hope International, takes a look at domestic minor sex trafficking, mingling the stories of young women with statistics on trafficking in the United States.

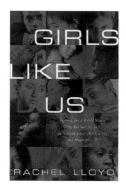

Girls Like Us
Rachel Lloyd

An excellent synopsis of sex trafficking among the young women of America. Lloyd weaves in her own gripping story of commercial sexual exploitation with compelling testimonies from the young women she counsels in New York, along with a practical viewpoint on what the American government is/isn't doing to protect and assist these girls.

Human Trafficking Handbook
The Salvation Army

A comprehensive study and analysis of human trafficking. This handbook covers the entire basics of what classifies as human trafficking, protection and programs available for trafficking victims, understanding the dynamics of control, how to identify a victim, and trauma-informed services to trafficking victims.

Resources

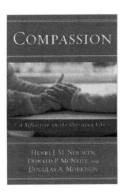

Compassion
Henri J.M. Nouwen, Donald P. Mcneill, Douglas A. Morrison

Exodus Cry's all-staff book choice for 2015, this tri-authored essay powerfully unpacks the compassion of Christ and the centralized role it must play in every believer's life.

The author challenges individuals to embrace the pain and sorrows of others and to truly live a compassionate life, in deep community with like-minded followers of Christ. For those involved in compassionate ministry, it is a must-read.

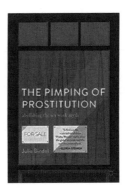

The Pimping of Prostitution:
Abolishing the Sex Work Myth
Julie Bindel

A compelling and significant must-read for every abolitionist looking to deepen their understanding of the different current international legislative models and the common myths and arguments surrounding the sex industry.

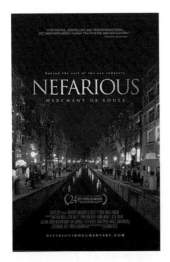

Nefarious
Merchant of Souls

Exodus Cry's own multi-award winning documentary exposes the disturbing trends of modern-day sex slavery. Shot in 19 countries, *Nefarious* exposes the nightmare of sex trafficking as experienced by hundreds of thousands daily, hearing the stories of both the enslaved and their traffickers. *Nefarious* features expert analysis from international humanitarian leaders and captures the gripping, triumphant testimonies of survivors to galvanize hope and vision.

Intervention Manual

Sex and Money

This documentary focuses on minor sex trafficking specifically in the United States, and the modern-day abolitionist movement fighting to stop it. Journey with a team of YWAM photojournalists as they travel in an RV across the nation, seeking to understand how the sexual exploitation of children has become the nation's fastest-growing form of organized crime, and how we should respond to this injustice.

MATTOO Manual

MATTOO's Education Program (MEP) is a manual designed to inform men in an engaging way about the myths and realities of sex trafficking. Ideal for men's small groups, the manual is a dynamically written and designed book that educates and empowers men to engage in the fight and bring cultural change.

Prostitution Narratives:
Stories of Survival in the Sex Trade by Caroline Norma and Melinda Tankard

For too long, the global sex industry and its vested interests have dominated the prostitution debate, repeating the antiquated line that "sex work is just like any job." Little is said of the damage, violation, suffering, and torment of prostitution on the bodies and minds of mostly women and children, nor of the deaths, suicides, and murders that have become routine in the sex industry. Through telling the experiences of real women who have survived prostitution, this book refutes the lies and debunks the myths.

Fallen
Out of the Sex Industry & Into the Arms of the Savior by Annie Lobert and A.J. Gregory

Annie Lobert gives a riveting and redemptive account of surviving 16 years in the sex industry in Las Vegas and the miraculous deliverance she experienced in the arms of Jesus. *Fallen* also sheds light on the complex exploitative relationship between a woman and her pimp and the other coercive and manipulative factors that keep women in prostitution. Today, Annie is redeemed, healed, and helping other victims of commercial sexual exploitation through her Las Vegas organization, Hookers for Jesus.

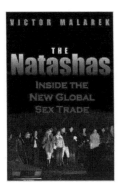

The Natashas
Victor Malarek

As an undercover journalist, Malarek takes a gritty look at the sex trafficking of European women. This book does end with a sense of hopelessness. Malarek's solution is not the solution that Exodus Cry stands behind; however, his investigative techniques and behind-the-scenes look at international sex trafficking are unparalleled. Malarek was featured in the Exodus Cry documentary *Nefarious: Merchant of Souls*.

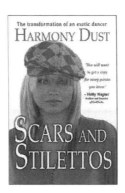

Scars and Stilettos
The Transformation of an Exotic Dancer by Harmony Dust

At 19, Harmony Dust ended up working as an exotic dancer in a fully nude strip club. Her sensitive, thoughtful writing style takes readers on a powerful journey from darkness into light. Harmony Dust now leads Treasures, an organization helping women in the sex trade, particularly those in strip clubs, discover their true worth. Her story is beautifully told and full of redemption found in Christ.

Roadmap to Redemption by Rebecca Bender

Designed for both survivors of sex trafficking and those who work closely alongside them in the field, this must-read workbook gives invaluable insight into trafficking in America: the psychological coercion and dynamics of the exploiter/exploited and the realities of walking the path of healing and restoration in Christ. Bender is a prominent survivor-leader in the anti-trafficking movement and works with survivors and organizations worldwide. She also serves on the board at Exodus Cry. For additional resources and training, see her organization's website, www.rebeccabender.org.

Resources

PART 4:
The Current Landscape of Exploitation

In the past, "trafficking" was usually defined as separate from "modern slavery." All human trafficking was a form of modern slavery, but not all of modern slavery was human trafficking.

Traditionally, movement has primarily defined the term "human trafficking." In recent years, however, particularly in 2011 and 2012, human trafficking has been primarily defined by exploitation. To be accurate in our presentations (oral or written), we must be clear about the definition of human trafficking we're using when we cite statistics. When talking about trafficking in terms of movement across international borders, we use different statistics than when we're talking about trafficking in terms of exploitation. The definitions created by the Palermo Protocols and the Trafficking Victims Protection Act (TVPA) require "physical transport."

(See Appendix H to read the United Nations-Protocol to Prevent, Suppress, and Punish Trafficking in Persons Especially Women and Children, supplementing the United Nations Convention against Transnational Organized Crime [Palermo Protocols].)

In the United States, the TVPA and its reauthorizations in 2003, 2005 and 2008 define human trafficking as:

- Sex trafficking in which a commercial sex act is induced by force, fraud, or coercion, or in which the person induced to perform such act has not attained 18 years of age.

- The recruitment, harboring, transportation, provision or obtaining of a person for labor or services, through the use of force, fraud or coercion for the purpose of subjection to involuntary servitude, peonage, debt bondage, or slavery.

Critical to this definition is recognizing that while trafficking often involves the movement of people from their own communities and transporting them across borders or within a nation, a victim does not need to be physically transported for this crime to fall under the TVPA definition. Additionally, the TVPA does not require force, fraud, or coercion when the commercial sex act involves a minor or someone under the age of 18. And finally, the TVPA recognizes international, or foreign-born, persons, as well as U.S. citizens and legal permanent residents, as potential victims of human trafficking.

The TVPA also addresses the subtle means of coercion that

Intervention Manual

traffickers use to control victims, including psychological coercion, trickery, and the seizure of documents—activities that were difficult to prosecute under pre-existing involuntary servitude statutes and case law.[3]

Below, we've listed detailed statistics from the United Nations Office on Drugs and Crime (UNODC) and the International Labor Organization (ILO) that you may find useful in presentations, educational workshops, grant writing, etc.

Trafficking as defined by movement across borders (UNODC):

- In 2009, the UNODC released the first global estimate of the scope of human trafficking, saying that 600,000 to 800,000 people are trafficked across international borders each year for any reason. Of those, 79 percent are used for commercial sexual exploitation.[4]

- We often hear people quote the stats, "There are 27 million slaves or victims of human trafficking in the world today," and "79 percent of all trafficking victims are trafficked for commercial sexual exploitation." Both figures are accurate, but when used together, they become incorrect.

Trafficking as defined by "exploitation":

On June 1, 2012, the International Labor Organization (ILO) released its second global estimate of forced labor—20.9 million victims. The 2012 U.S. Trafficking in Persons Report used these statistics as the new global estimate. Given the current availability of data, the ILO believes its methodology to be the best available. The ILO report is now regarded as the most accurate source:

- Sexual exploitation = 4.5 million

- Labor exploitation = 14.2 million

- State-imposed forced labor = 2.2 million

- The ILO's first estimate of forced labor in 2005 was 12.3 million victims of forced labor and sex trafficking. Unlike the 2005 estimate, the new 2012 finding does not separate human trafficking victims as a subset of the global forced labor estimate

- but instead recognizes that human trafficking is now defined by exploitation, not by movement.[5]

- Many people ask why Exodus Cry focuses on women and girls. The answer is simple. According to the ILO's 2012 estimate, 55 percent of forced labor victims are women and girls, as are 98 percent of all victims of sex trafficking.

- The Asia and Pacific region (which includes South Asia) remains the region with the largest number of victims, though the number of trafficking victims in Africa has grown considerably since the 2005 estimate.

On February 12, 2013, the UNODC released its newest Global Report on Trafficking in Persons Report. Key findings include:

- Some 136 different nationalities were trafficked and detected in 118 different countries.

- Trafficking for sexual exploitation is more common in Europe, Central Asia, and the Americas. Trafficking for forced labor is more frequently detected in Africa and the Middle East, as well as in South and East Asia and the Pacific.

- Trafficking for the purpose of sexual exploitation accounts for 58 percent of all trafficking cases detected globally, while trafficking for forced labor accounts for 36 percent.

Please note: The officially reported information that forms the basis of this 2013 global report cannot be used to generate a global estimate of the number of victims. The report has shed light on the patterns and flows of human trafficking. However, the UNODC report did point to the ILO report as the appropriate source for a global estimate.

Terminology

The words we use matter. Vocabulary reflects both accuracy and attitudes, specifically in our communication related to trafficking and prostitution. The subtle nuances (for example, prostitute vs. prostituted) can speak large volumes as we educate others and advocate for victims. On the next page, we've listed several terms and their definitions to help you understand where and when to use each one.

"issue" vs. "injustice"

- Issue: a matter in dispute between two or more parties; a vital or unsettled matter; concern, problem, the point at which an unsettled matter is ready for a decision.

- Injustice: the absence of justice; violation of right or of the rights of another; unfairness; an unjust act; wrong.

"sex work" vs. "prostitution"

- You can most likely tell someone's views on prostitution by the terms they use. As an organization subscribing to the "abolitionist" legal framework in dealing with sex trafficking and prostitution, we should never call prostitution "sex work." Some survivors prefer the term "commercial sexual exploitation" to prostitution as it outlines the harmful exploitive aspect of the sex trade.

"prostitute" vs. "prostituted"

- Prostitution is something that happens to a person; it is not who/what they are. "Prostitute," the noun, misleadingly equates who these people are with what is being done to them, while "prostituted" highlights the other people and social forces that are acting upon them.

Human Trafficking and Prostitution Are Inseparable

While some non-governmental organizations (NGOs), independent organizations, and government bodies try to separate prostitution and human trafficking, there is a growing awakening that human trafficking and prostitution are linked and thus are inseparable. Few women seek out or choose to be in prostitution, and most are desperate to leave it. A 2003 scientific study published in the *Journal of Trauma Practice* found that 89 percent of women in prostitution want to escape prostitution but had no other options for survival—offering a strong argument against the legalization of prostitution.

Researcher Melissa Farley wrote: "Prostitution and sex trafficking are linked. Sex trafficking happens when and where there is a demand for prostitution and a context of impunity for its customers. Legal prostitution sanitizes prostitution, making the harms of trafficking for prostitution invisible. Suddenly, dirty money becomes clean. Illegal acts become legal. Overnight, pimps are transformed into legitimate businessmen and ordinary entrepreneurs, and men who would not formerly consider buying a woman in prostitution think, *Well, if it's legal, now it must be okay.*"[6]

Addressing prostitution is a must for those fighting sex trafficking because sex trafficking is a matter of supply and demand. In the documentary *Nefarious: Merchant of Souls*, Exodus Cry Founder and President Benjamin Nolot asks Victor Malarek, a Canadian journalist reporting on human trafficking: "Why are girls being trafficked?"

Malarek: "Because there is a demand. They wouldn't be trafficked if there were no demand. The girls are the supply side; the women are the supply side. You can build the best mousetrap factory in the world. If you have no mice, what the heck do you need a mousetrap factory for… the reason we have this problem is because of demand. The girls are the supply side. The men are the demand side—very, very basic Economics 101 here. You cannot have supply without demand, but in this issue demand has three key letters in it: M-A-N."[7]

The U.S. Government: Prostitution Fuels Human Trafficking

In November 2008, Ambassador Mark Lagon, director of the U.S. Office to Monitor and Combat Trafficking in Persons, addressed conference attendees in Berne, Switzerland, to share the United States' position on the overlaps of prostitution, migration and human trafficking. Below, we've excerpted from his speech (italics added):

"Two years after the enactment of the TVPA, the U.S. government adopted a strong position against prostitution in a December 2002 policy decision, which notes that prostitution is inherently harmful and dehumanizing and fuels trafficking in persons.

"Turning people into dehumanized commodities creates an enabling environment for human trafficking. The U.S. government opposes prostitution and any related activities, including pimping, pandering, or maintaining brothels as contributing to the phenomenon of trafficking in persons. These activities should not be regulated as a legitimate form of work for any human being.

"This policy represents a significant paradigm shift. U.S. policy now categorizes prostitution as primarily a harmful phenomenon rather than a neutral work choice or market transaction. Why? Because prostitution fuels human trafficking. Because few activities are as brutal and as damaging to people as prostitution. And because organized crime networks do not protect prostituted people."[8]

Additionally, the 2007 Trafficking in Persons Report stated that, "sex trafficking would not exist without the demand for commercial sex flourishing around the world. Prostitution and related activities—including pimping and patronizing or maintaining brothels—encourage the growth of modern-day slavery by providing a facade or background where traffickers operate. Where prostitution is tolerated, there is a greater demand for human trafficking victims and nearly always an increase in the number of women and children trafficked into commercial sex slavery."

PART 5:
Legal Approaches To Prostitution Legislation Worldwide

Throughout the world, prostitution is viewed and treated differently. Below we've summarized the various approaches to prostitution based on the global area. Notice how the terms change according to the approach to legislation.

Legalization - Netherlands / Australia (Victoria) / Nevada

- In these areas, prostitution is legal and is redefined as "sex work." Regulations control the when, where, and how of the provision of sexual services. (Some aspects of prostitution can be criminalized.) In Nevada, the state collects tax revenue on income associated with prostitution.

- Terms used in these areas: prostituted women = sex workers; purchasers of sex acts = clients; pimps = managers; brothel owners = business people; traffickers = employment or travel agents who assist migrant sex workers.

Decriminalization - New Zealand / Australia (New South Wales)

- These areas have seen a complete removal of prostitution and related activities from the criminal code. Prostitution/brothels are treated as any other business or form of work. Prostitution has been redefined as "sex work." Pro-prostitution groups favor complete decriminalization.

- Terms used in these areas: prostituted women = sex workers; purchasers of sex acts = clients; pimps = managers; brothel owners = business people; traffickers = employment or travel agents who assist migrant sex workers.

Criminalization/prohibition – United States/Middle East (with the exception of Israel)

- In these areas, prostitution is a criminal activity, and all aspects are criminalized (buying, selling, pimping [procuring and pandering], and brothels). These areas adhere to prohibition in law, but often exhibit tolerance in practice. The laws are gender-neutral, but women are arrested the majority of the time. Children are often arrested and treated as criminals.

Abolition - Sweden/Norway/Iceland/Canada/Northern Ireland/France

- In these areas, prostitution is considered a form of violence against women and not a legitimate form of work for any human being. The purchase of sex is criminalized along with pimping, trafficking, and brothel keeping. These areas recognize the connection between human trafficking and prostitution with a focus on reducing "demand."

- Terms used in these areas: prostitution = exploitation; prostituted persons = victims of violence and exploitation; pimps, johns, and traffickers = perpetrators (criminals).

The Prostitution Debate

The debate (and usually the law as well) is organized by five underlying moral distinctions that divide the terrible from the tolerable: 1) adult is distinguished from child prostitution; 2) indoor from outdoor (also called "underground" or "below the law"); 3) legal from illegal; 4) voluntary from forced; and 5) prostitution from trafficking.

In a speech in Bihar, India, author and activist Catherine McKinnon spoke about these five distinctions: "It is said that child prostitution is always bad for children; adult prostitution is not always bad for adults. Outdoor prostitution can be rough; indoor prostitution is less so. Illegal prostitution has problems that legal prostitution solves. Forced prostitution is bad; voluntary prostitution can be not so bad. Trafficking is really, really bad. Prostitution—if, say, voluntary, indoor, legal, adult—can be a tolerable life for some people. Measured against known facts of the sex trade, these purported distinctions emerge as largely illusory. These moral distinctions have consequences for law, policy, and culture that are real."[9]

"Sex Work" Model vs. "Sexual Exploitation" Model

The "sex work" approach favors across-the-board decriminalization with various forms of legalization.

"Sex work" model: In this model, prostitution is viewed as and is called "the oldest profession." It is consensual because paid;

stigmatized because illegal; a form of sexual liberation; and a choice a woman makes.

The goal with this model is to remove criminal sanctions from all actors in the sex industry so that prostitution becomes as legitimate as any other job or business. The Netherlands, Germany, New Zealand, Victoria in Australia, as well as 10 counties in the U.S. state of Nevada, have all adopted versions of this approach, although some, such as the Netherlands, are retreating from it.[10]

"Sexual exploitation" model: In this model, prostitution is viewed as and called "the oldest oppression," a form of violence against women and the resort of those with the fewest or no choices when all else fails. Sweden, Norway, Iceland, Canada, Northern Ireland and France have all adopted versions of this approach.

"The coercion (physical and psychological force) behind prostitution produces an economic sector of sexual abuse. The money coerces the sex rather than guaranteeing consent to it, making prostitution a practice of serial rape. In this analysis, there is, and can be, nothing equal about it...In this view, people in prostitution are wrongly saddled with a stigma that properly belongs to their exploiters."[11]

In the sexual exploitation model, usually the method of abolition champions the "Swedish model" or the "Nordic model," now called the "Equality Model," which criminalizes the purchase, but not the sale, of sex. The sexual exploitation approach seeks to abolish prostitution.

Common Arguments for Legalizing Prostitution (and Why They Don't Work)

- If you make prostitution illegal, it will go "underground": The argument that criminalizing the purchase of sex will drive it underground is not based on any evidence. To the contrary, in Sweden and Norway, criminalizing the purchase of sex reduced the number of men purchasing prostituted women, thus less women were prostituting on the whole.

Because the nature of prostitution is such that it must be visible to the clients who purchase the women, it is not possible for prostitution to go so far underground as to be undetected. If the men who

Intervention Manual

purchase women are able to find the women, then trained police surely can as well. The people who argue against criminalization because it will drive prostitution underground are the same people who argue that brothels should be legal because they believe indoor prostitution is safer than street prostitution.

- Proponents of the "sex work" model say that legal/decriminalized prostitution will enable women to have better health, safer working environments, and that it will help prevent HIV/AIDS and STDs because the women won't be afraid to carry condoms, ask for help from police if they're in danger, or seek help from health professionals.

But when prostitution is viewed as "commercial sexual exploitation" instead of "sex work," we understand that the resulting cases of diseases and HIV/AIDS are a symptom, the cause of which is prostitution itself (sex with thousands of men a year under conditions you cannot realistically control.)[12]

The "sex work" perspective protects johns from the prostituted women so they can keep using them without becoming ill, rather than protecting the women from the buyers who are giving them life-threatening diseases and psychological trauma. Example: Health cards are given to women so they can present them to the buyers. However, buyers never have health check cards to present to the women.

Many tests take several days/weeks to get results. During that time, women see more men who could be infected. STD health checks cannot reasonably detect/protect against STDs. Furthermore, throughout the world, study after study documents that about half of all johns request or insist that condoms are not used when they purchase sex. This argument also fails to take into consideration that no matter how many condoms are used or how many health checks a woman gets, she cannot be protected from post-traumatic stress disorder (PTSD) and the physiological/emotional harm that 68 percent of all prostituted women will face. The "sex work" argument does not take mental/emotional/spiritual health into consideration. *The only way to truly protect the health of a prostituted woman is to get her out of prostitution.*

- A common mindset advocating legalization says that nothing is fundamentally problematic about prostitution itself. There is no intrinsic harm in prostitution; it is just consensual sex for money. The first fault line in the denial of intrinsic harm appears when it is universally agreed that children should not be prostituted. Why not? If there is no inherent harm in prostitution and if it is just like any other job, why is it forbidden for children?"

What happens to the nature of prostitution during the 24 hours between when a child is 17 and when she is 18 years old? When did they change from being victims of human trafficking to being consenting adults? At what point does a person stop being a victim of human trafficking and turn into a "sex worker?" Prostituted women are prostituted children who were lucky enough to live long enough to become women. They are not two separate groups of people; they are the same group of people at different times in their lives."[13]

Legalization and Decriminalization Increases Prostitution, Illegal Activity, Organized Crime, and Human Trafficking

- Research indicates that legal prostitution increases organized crime and human trafficking. In 2012, researchers Seo-Young Cho, Axel Dreher, and Eric Neumayer published a quantitative, empirical analysis of a cross-section of up to 150 countries. The analysis revealed that on average, countries with legalized prostitution experience a larger degree of human trafficking inflows.[14]

- In 2008, eight years after the removal of a brothel ban in the Netherlands, the Dutch National Police carried out the SchoneSchiin study, detailing the role of human trafficking in the legalized prostitution sector. Researchers estimated that 50 to 90 percent of women in legalized prostitution were "working involuntarily." Based on these estimates, the Amsterdam legal brothel sector alone would "employ" 4,000 victims of human trafficking annually.

- In his research, "The Legitimization of Prostitutes and Its Impact on Trafficking in Women and Children," (2005), sociology professor Richard Poulin wrote:

"Although there was a belief that legalization would make possible the control of the sex industry, the illegal industry is now 'out of control.' Police in Victoria [Australia] estimate that there are 400 illegal brothels versus 100 legal ones. Trafficking in women and children from other countries has increased significantly. The legalization of prostitution in some parts of Australia has thus resulted in a net growth of the industry. One of the results has been the trafficking in women and children to 'supply' legal and illegal brothels. The 'sex entrepreneurs' have difficulty recruiting women locally to supply an expanding industry, and women from trafficking are more vulnerable and more profitable."[15]

- After the legalization of prostitution in New South Wales in 1995, brothels tripled in number by 1999 and expanded in size, the vast majority having no licenses but operating and advertising with impunity.

The Nordic Model of Legislation (Supported by Exodus Cry)

"I believe that we will never succeed in combating trafficking in women if we do not simultaneously work to abolish prostitution and the sexual exploitation of women and children." —Margareta Winberg, former deputy prime minister of Sweden

Sweden[16]

On January 1, 1999, Sweden became the first country in the world to introduce legislation criminalizing the purchase—but not the sale of—sexual services. The most important insight was that attention must be directed to the purchasers—a shift in perspective, which can be summarized by stating the obvious: If there were no demand, there would be no prostitution.

Sex purchase laws in Sweden constitute a progressive legislative approach, recognizing the fact that legal prostitution fuels human trafficking; that prostitution is inherently harmful; and that an overall reduction or total elimination of the number of people for sale should be the goal of prostitution legislation. This approach recognizes that the ones with the most choices (the buyers, pimps, and traffickers) are the ones who should be punished for exploitation, and those with the least choice or no choice (prostituted women, men, and children) should be offered help and services for escape from the sex industry.

Since the introduction of the ban on the purchase of sexual services, street prostitution in Sweden has been reduced by 50 percent. In comparison, before the ban on the purchase of sexual services was introduced in Sweden, the prevalence of street prostitution was about the same in the three capital cities of Norway, Denmark, and Sweden. The number of women in street prostitution in both Norway and Denmark subsequently increased dramatically after the legislation passed in Sweden. (Note: The increase in neighboring countries did not equal the decrease in Sweden and therefore could not be the result of it.) Less than 7.8 percent of Sweden's active adult male population buys sex now as compared to 13.6 percent before the law was passed and implemented.

In 2008, the number of people in street prostitution in both Norway and Denmark was estimated to be three times higher than in Sweden. In light of the three countries' great economic and social similarities, we can assume that the reduction in street prostitution in Sweden is a direct result of criminalization.

To gauge Swedish public opinion concerning sex purchases, surveys were conducted before and after criminalization was introduced. Judging by the results of four population-based opinion polls, there has been a change of attitude with regard to the purchase of sexual services that coincides with the criminalization of the purchase of such services. The marked shift in attitude—without an equivalent shift in Norway and Denmark—must be interpreted to mean that the ban itself has had a significant normative effect. Given that support for criminalization is greatest among young people, that ban can be expected to last. In all three surveys conducted since the ban was introduced, more than 70 percent of those surveyed took a positive view of it.

The Swedish law stands upon the belief that prostitution is a serious barrier to gender equality and that any society claiming to defend principles of equality must reject the idea that women and girls are commodities that can be bought, sold, and sexually exploited by men.

This victim-centered approach recognizes that prostitution is not about the commodification of sex and of people, but is actually a manifestation of sex inequality. Across the world, women are the vast majority of those being sold into prostitution and men are those buying.

Norway

On January 1, 2009, Norway followed Sweden's lead and adopted legislation explicitly criminalizing the purchase of sex. After the law went into effect, Norway saw a dramatic reduction in both indoor and outdoor prostitution.

According to the country's government-funded Pro Centre report, "Many people, including Pro Centre, predicted a decline in overall prostitution after it was made illegal to buy sex. We were right. Some people, but not Pro Centre, predicted that women would flow from the streets to the indoor market. That did not turn out to be the case."

After the law was enacted for the whole of Norway, the number of prostitution-related advertisements fell by 28 percent. Because advertisements are necessary for buyers to find the women, "underground" or "indoor" prostitution in Norway could not have increased.

From 2008 through 2009, prostitution overall (indoor and outdoor) was reduced by 50 percent, and the number of women on the streets in the capital city of Oslo was also halved. The number of women in indoor prostitution in Oslo fell by 16 percent, and in the whole of Norway, indoor prostitution was reduced by 19 percent in 2009.

Based on the evidence of positive results due to the sex purchase laws in the Nordic countries of Sweden, Norway, and Iceland, many other countries are looking into adopting similar measures to combat human trafficking and the prostitution industry. Northern Ireland and Canada implemented this legislation in 2014.

In the last few years, the Nordic-model style of legislation has also been discussed in the parliaments of France, Ireland, Scotland, England, and Wales. In early 2014, the parliaments of the European Union and the Council of Europe both adopted non-binding resolutions recommending member states consider the Nordic model. An increasing number of activists and organizations across the globe (many of which are survivor-led) in countries such as South Africa, India, Lebanon, Germany, Denmark, Austria, New Zealand, and the United States, are calling for lawmakers to recognize the realities of prostitution and to enact the Nordic model.[17]

In the United States, in 2007 New York moved toward the Swedish model by legislating penalties for buyers higher than those for prostituted people, by creating the class B felony for "sex trafficking," and by excluding victims from accomplice liability for trafficking. But the sold remained criminals (deeming "prostitution" a class B misdemeanor). This is the Nordic model lite: harsher penalties for johns (jail time); lighter penalties for prostituted women; education of law enforcement (paradigm shift); and a recognition of prostitution as a form of violence against women.

Note: Exodus Cry favors abolition and would be considered an abolitionist organization.

Resources

SECTION 6:
Endnotes and Appendix

164

Endnotes

APPENDIX A

169

Texting Scripts

APPENDIX B

179

Setting Up Google Voice

APPENDIX C

180

Sexual Intregrity Commitment Form

APPENDIX D

181

Confidentiality Form

APPENDIX E

185

Reporting Forms

APPENDIX F

186

Meeting Form

APPENDIX G

188

History Form

APPENDIX H

191

Palermo Protocols

Endnotes

Section 1: Intervention 101

[1] *Nefarious: Merchant of Souls* (DVD) Exodus Cry, Kansas City, Kan., 2012.

[2] Prostitution Facts, rapeis.org, http://www.rapeis.org/activism/prostitution/prostitutionfacts.html.

[3] Malika Saada Saar, "Stopping the Foster Care to Child Trafficking Pipeline," (Oct. 29 2013), http://www.huffingtonpost.com/malika-saada-saar/stopping-the-foster-care-_b_4170483.html.

[4] Kathleen Barry, *The Prostitution of Sexuality* (1996), NYU Press, New York.

[5] Vednita Carter, "Prostitution: Where Racism and Sexism Intersect," (1993) *Michigan Journal of Gender & Law*. Also see Melissa Farley, Jacqueline Lynne & Ann J. Cotton, "Prostitution in Vancouver: Violence and the Colonization of First Nations Women, Transcultural Psychiatry" (2005) http://www.prostitutionresearch.com/pdfs/ProstVancouver.pdf

[6] Rachel Moran, 2014, www.theprostitutionexperience.com

[7] Dorchen A. Leidholdt, "Prostitution and Trafficking in Women: An Intimate Relationship," (2003), http://www.prostitutionresearch.com/Leidholdt%20Prostitution%20and%20Trafficking%20in%20Women.pdf

[8] Duren Banks and Tracey Kyckelhahn, "Characteristics of Suspected Human Trafficking Incidents, 2008-2010," U.S. Department of Justice.

Section 2: Online Exploitation

[1] Douglas Dowty, "Syracuse Police Charge 36 in Prostitution Sting Originating on Internet," syracuse.com (Dec. 7, 2012), http://www.syracuse.com/news/index.ssf/2011/04/syracuse_police_charge_36_in_p.html

[2] See Melissa Farley et al., "Comparing Sex Buyers With Men Who Don't Buy Sex" (2011), http://www.prostitutionresearch.com/pdfs/Farleyetal2011ComparingSexBuyers.pdf

[3] See Bill McAllister, "From Streetwalking to the Information Superhighway: The New Method in Prostitution," Police Prostitution & Politics (July 30, 2011).

[4] Victor Malarek, *The Johns: Sex for Sale and the Men Who Buy It*, Arcade Publishing, New York, 2009, p.103

[5] See stats from Paint Bottle quoted on HuffPost: http://www.huffingtonpost.com/2013/05/03/internet-porn-stats_n_3187682.html

[6] https://www.webroot.com/us/en/home/resources/tips/digital-family-life/internet-pornography-by-the-numbers

[7] According to Kassia Wosick, assistant professor of sociology at New Mexico State University.
See http://www.nbcnews.com/business/business-news/things-are-looking-americas-porn-industry-n289431

[8] Melissa Farley, Kenneth Franzblau and M. Alexis Kennedy, "Online Prostitution and Trafficking," (2014) http://prostitutionresearch.com/pub_author/melissa-farley-and-kenneth-franzblau-and-m-alexis-kennedy

[9] Ibid. p.129

[10] Angie Jackson, "Prostitution: Internet Classifieds Create Element of Secrecy, Challenge for Grand Rapids Police," MLIVE (Nov. 17, 2013) http://www.mlive.com/news/grandrapids/index.ssf/2013/11/internet.html

[11] J. Potterat, D. Brewer, S. Muth, R. Rothenberg, D. Woodhouse, J. Muth, H. Stite, and S. Brody, "Mortality in a Long-Term Open Cohort of Prostitute Women," American Journal of Epidemiology 159:pp. 778–785, (2004)

[12] Ibid

[13] Raymond, J., D'Cunha, J., Dzuhayatin, S. R., Hynes, H. P., Ramirez Rodriguez, Z., and Santos, A. (2002). N. Amherst, Mass.: Coalition Against Trafficking in Women (CATW).

[14] Melissa Farley, Kenneth Franzblau and M. Alexis

Kennedy, "Online Prostitution and Trafficking," 2014 http://prostitutionresearch.com/pub_author/melissa-farley-and-kenneth-franzblau-and-m-alexis-kennedy/

[15] Jennifer Quinn & Robert Cribb, "Inside the World of Human Trafficking," Toronto Star, (Oct. 5, 2013) available at https://www.thestar.com/news/gta/2013/10/05/inside_the_world_of_human_sex_trafficking.html

[16] See generally Melissa Farley et al., "Attitudes and Social Characteristics of Men Who Buy Sex in Scotland," 3 Psychol.. Trauma: Theory, Res., Prac., and Pol'y pp. 369, 375 (2011)

[17] See Blevins and Holt, supra note 18, at p. 635.

[18] Melissa Farley, Kenneth Franzblau and M. Alexis Kennedy, "Online Prostitution and Trafficking" 2014, http://prostitutionresearch.com/pub_author/melissa-farley-and-kenneth-franzblau-and-m-alexis-kennedy/

[19] "Online Prostitution Ads Generated at Least $37.3 Million in Last Year," AIM GROUP (Oct. 25, 2012), https://www.aimgroup.com/2013/07/10/online-prostitution-ad-revenue-crosses-craigslist-benchmark/

[20] Ibid.

[21] "Online Prostitution-Ad Revenue Crosses Craigslist Benchmark," AIM GROUP (July 10, 2013), https://www.aimgroup.com/2013/07/10/online-prostitution-ad-revenue-crosses-craigslist-benchmark/

[22] Sara Jean Green, "The Weekly, Its Parent Company Face Backlash Over Online Sex Ads That Exploit Teens," *The Seattle Times* (July 23, 2011) http://www.seattletimes.com/seattle-news/the-weekly-its-parent-company-face-backlash-over-online-sex-ads-that-exploit-teens/

[23] Nicholas Kristof, "Where Pimps Peddle Their Goods", *The New York Times* (March 17 2012) https://www.nytimes.com/2012/03/18/opinion/sunday/kristof-where-pimps-peddle-their-goods.html

[24] Cook County Sheriff's Office, "Sheriff Dart's Demand to Defund Sex Trafficking Compels Visa and Mastercard to Sever Ties with

Backpage.com"(July 1, 2015) https://www.cookcountysheriff.org/sheriff-darts-demand-defund-sex-trafficking-compels-visa-master-card-sever-ties-backpage-com/

Section 5: Resources

[1] Courtois, C. A., Ford, J. D., & Herman, J. L. (2009). "Treating Complex Traumatic Stress Disorders: Evidence-Based Guide." Guilford Press, New York City

[2] Wilder, E. J. (1999). *The Red Dragon Cast Down: A redemptive response to the occult and Satanism*, Chosen Books, Grand Rapids, Mich.

[3] Joy M. Braun, "Collaborations: The Key to Combating Human Trafficking, " The Police Chief 70 (December 2003): 68–74.

[4] UNODC Global Report on Trafficking in Persons 2009

[5] U.S. Trafficking in Persons Report 2012

[6] Farley, Melissa et al. 2003. "Prostitution and Trafficking in Nine Countries: An Update on Violence and Posttraumatic Stress Disorder." Journal of Trauma Practice, Vol. 2, No. 3/4: 33-74; and Farley, Melissa. ed. 2003. *Prostitution, Trafficking, and Traumatic Stress*. Haworth Press, New York.

[7] *Nefarious: Merchant of Souls* (DVD) Exodus Cry, Kansas City, Kan., 2012, documentary interview footage

[8] "Overlaps of Prostitution, Migration and Human Trafficking" Ambassador Mark P. Lagon, director of the Office to Monitor and Combat Trafficking in Persons Berne, Switzerland (November 12, 2008) http://2001-2009.state.gov/g/tip/rls/rm/2008/111997.htm

[9] Catherine Mackinnon, "Trafficking, Prostitution, and Inequality", Copyright Catharine A. MacKinnon 2009, 2010, 2, speech, Bihar, India

[10] Ibid.

[11] Ibid.

[12] Ibid.

[13] Ibid.

[14] Seo-Young Cho, Axel Dreher, Eric Neumayer, "Does Legalized Prostitution Increase Human Trafficking?" September 2011 (updated January 2012) Courant Research Centre 'Poverty, Equity, and Growth in Developing and Transition Countries: Statistical Methods and Empirical Analysis' Georg-August – UniversitätGöttingen

[15] Richard Poulin, PhD, Professor of Sociology at the University of Ottawa, "The Legalization of Prostitution and Its Impact on Trafficking in Women and Children" (2005).

[16] Selected extracts of the Swedish government report SOU 2010:49: "The Ban Against The Purchase of Sexual Services. An evaluation 1999-2008 Swedish Institute & Ministry of Justice." Also see "The Swedish Law That Prohibits the Purchase of Sexual Services Best Practices for Prevention of Prostitution and Trafficking in Human Beings," Gunilla Eckberg, Ministry of Industry, Employment, and Communications. Violence Against Women, Vol. 10, No. 10, October 2004 1187-1218 DOI: 10.1177/1077801204268647 2004. Also see "Targeting the Sex Buyer The Swedish Example: Stopping Prostitution And Trafficking Where it All Begins." Kajsa Claude 2010 The Swedish Institute. Selected extracts of the Swedish government report SOU 2010:49: "The Ban Against The Purchase of Sexual Services. An evaluation 1999-2008." Swedish Institute 2010

[17] http://www.equalitynow.org/sites/default/files/Nordic_Model_EN.pdf

APPENDIX A
Texting Scripts

Below are some examples of real-life (unedited) texting conversations with exploited women. These scripts are meant to be used as a general guideline rather than a strict template, as everyone's texting style is slightly different. Keep in mind that you may need to adjust your style based on cues you may be receiving. For one woman, a direct approach might be best. For another, asking direct questions might be considered offensive. We need the Lord to guide us as we text.

Texting is a trial-and-error process. In our experiences, we used a texting pseudonym organization called Beauty Breakthrough. Exodus Cry has a strong anti-trafficking presence online, and we didn't want the women we were texting to feel intimidated.

Monica

Helen: Hi Monica! How's it going? :-) If u had alternatives would u wanna get out of the game? 3:34 PM
Monica: I do this to survive. And yes i want out i want out bad. 3:35 PM
Monica: Who is this and why are you asking me? 3:37 PM
Helen: So my name is Helen and im a volunteer with a few other women, we r called beauty breakthrough. We meet up with girls on Backpage and if they want out, we help them depending on where they r at. We just do it coz we really care about the girls and know many want out and so we see if we can help make it happen. Is this something ud be interested in? We cud talk on the phone if you'd prefer. Or text :) 3:42 PM
Helen: If u cud do any job what wud be ur dream? 3:43 PM
Monica: To be a teacher or counselor of some sort 3:44 PM
Helen: That's awesome!! I can c u having a caring heart that wants to help and teach others. Would you be up for talking on the phone? :-) 3:48 PM

2 days later:

Helen: Hey is this Monica? 4:13 PM
Monica: Sure is. Who's this? 4:38 PM
Helen: This is Helen from beauty breakthrough...we were texting the other day but then i didn't hear back so wanted to check u were still using this number. 4:42 PM
Helen: We text girls off Backpage and see if they r interested in

Appendix

meeting up to talk about their life options/particularly if they want out...We also give free beauty bags full of cosmetics and toiletries etc. Wud u be interested in getting one? 4:44 PM
Helen: There's no pressure and totally feel free to say no. It's just our way of reaching out and letting the girls know we care. 4:47 PM
Helen: What do u think? :-) 5:26 PM
Monica: Of course i do. 7:32 PM
Monica: How do i sign up? 7:39 PM
Helen: :-) great. Well is there any public place or cafe ud feel comfortable meeting at? We cud meet tomorrow or fri afternoon? And we usually just give u the purse (it has some great stuff in it) and talk thru anything u want. Does that sound good? Helen :-) 8:20 PM
Monica: Sounds great. I cud meet you somewhere but i will have someone with me because of obvious reasons. 8:23 PM
Monica: Your program sounds great but i am a little skeptical just saying. Please dont take offense. If this is ok lets set up time n place 8:24 PM
Helen: Don't worry i totally understand. I am in NO way trying to recruit u. And we always meet in a public place so the girls feel safe etc. I'm just a girl who does this voluntarily with a few others to reach out to the girls we c on backpage. We want them to know ppl care about them n r there for them! 8:31 PM
Helen: So is there like a mcdonalds or cafe near u that's good? What area in kc are you? 8:32 PM
Helen: Wud tomorrow at 2pm work?? Or same time friday. It wud just be me and another girl meeting you. 8:43 PM

5 days later:

Helen: Hey Monica its Helen remember we were texting the other week about giving u a free beauty bag? Wud u still like one? :-) 5:19 PM
Monica: Of course 7:18 PM
Helen: Great :-) they r really nice. Where abouts in kc are u at? We (another female volunteer and i) could meet u in a fast food place somewhere u know to give it to u. 7:27 PM
Monica: Ok tonight? 7:40 PM
Helen: Are u free tomorrow afternoon? 7:42 PM
Monica: Maybe its better to ask like day of. im busy alot 7:43 PM
Helen: Yeah i understand...well shall i text u tomorrow and we'll c if ur free in the afternoon :-)
The next day:

Helen: Glad u were able to come meet us tonight. I've been thinking and praying for u since and hope ur doing ok? Did u look in the purse? :-) xx12:00 AM

Monica: Helen im just now getting my phone turned on. you are an angel and a true blessing to have experienced. thanks so much for your nonjudgmental generosity. hope you have a wonderful nite. 1:25 AM

Hailey

Helen: Hey is this Hailey??
Hailey: Yes whos this
Helen: hi how ru! my name is helen :)
Helen: i saw ur ad on backpage a while back. i volunteer for beauty breakthrough, u know about it?
Helen: i meet with girls on bp and give them a free beauty bag with a ton of beauty products as a free gift just to show we care.
Helen: if the girl wants out or wants to know any other options or is in a tough spot, then we are totally there for her. if not, that's ok too and we just give u the free bag as a gift. usually just meet in a public place like a fast food place. wud u like one? :)
Hailey: Yes. I would. Where would we meet and where r u guys from.
Helen: Ok great :-) we r in south kc, what about u? Is there a cafe or fast food place near u that we cud meet u in? What's ur schedule today looking like? :)
Hailey: Well im in nkc and im actually on house arrest, I will be off on monday so that might work out better for me unless u would wanna meet on saturday
Hailey: And u keep saying we??? How many people are coming???
Helen: Sorry yes that might sound intimidating! It wud just be me and one other volunteer. We do meetings in pairs, makes more sense. Monday is good for me too actually. That's fine for me to drive to nkc :-) is 2pm a good time for u? What r ur restrictions for leaving the house at the moment? or did u mean ur off house arrest by monday? :)
Hailey: Maybe u can meet me at hyvee or walmart if thats convenient for you

Helen: Yes that would work. Maybe Hyvee as it has a cafe and we could have coffee or lunch together before you shop and we could give u the beauty bag :) Which hyvee is the one u go to?
Hailey: Well I go to the one off 64th and i29 hwy
Helen: Ok cool, well shall we arrange to meet you at the cafe there at 2pm on Monday?
Helen: I will give you a little call sometime before then so you can hear my voice and be reassured i'm legit and not law enforcement etc, ifyou had any concerns (some girls r worried we r, but we r not affiliated with that in any form)
Hailey: Well, my only question is y if u people I guess are doin this and is this a group of people doing this and why who funds u and theres a lot of red flags kinda, just kinda let me in on the business and what not
Helen: Valid questions which I'm glad ur asking :-) we r connected to and partly funded by a larger org that helps women. But we all just do this in r spare time so a lot of the volunteers have other jobs too. Let me just call u :-)

Peachez

Helen: Hey is this Peachez? 2:21 PM
Peachez: Yes it is and this is? 2:22 PM
Helen: Hi! How ru doing? 2:25 PM
Peachez: I'm good thanks how bout yourself 2:33 PM
Helen: i'mgood thanks! :) i saw ur ad on bp...i'm called helen, with beauty breakthrough have u heard of it? 2:46 PM
Peachez: Are you a cop or work with any law enforcement in any way 2:46 PM
Helen: its a small nonprofit, not connected to any law enforcement no. I meet with girls on backpage and escorting sites to give u more life options and give out free beauty bags with a load of beauty products. There's no pressure we just wanna bless u with a beauty bag as a free gift and make sure u have r contact details for the future :-) so u know u have someone in kc who is there 4u 2:50 PM
Peachez: Such as if you don't mind me asking when it comes to options and connect in what way what is it that your asking of me? 2:50 PM
Helen: Not asking anything of u, more that u can ask something of us :) the beauty bag is not dependent on whether u wanna come out of the game or not, we just wanna connect with u so u have

our details and we can bless u with a bag :) We have resources and connections with things like jobs, education, college, clothes, counseling, accommodation, stuff for kids if u have any. But that is entirely up to u whether u want help with any of this stuff. if not, let us just take u for coffee :) 2:54 PM

Helen: What do u think? do u have any questions?? :) 2:57 PM

Peachez: I can't today I'm at the hospital but I do appreciate it that would be wonderful 2:57 PM

Helen: I'm glad u are up for meeting :) We just wanna be a blessing and it sounds like it's come at a good time - ru free tomorrow any time? We usually just go for a coffee at a local fast food or cafe :) Hope ur doing ok at the hospital 3:01 PM

Peachez: I have ink poisoning in my leg and its made me sick with sores everywhere but ill be ok thanks for the concern 3:01 PM

Helen: Aw no that sounds painful!! is there anything particular you need or have they got it covered at the hospital? 3:02 PM

Peachez: I might have to stay over night but I think ill be ok that's nice of you though thank you 3:03 PM

Helen: Hope u can sleep....hospitals can be rough for overnight stays sometimes. 3:04 PM

Peachez: Yeah tell me about it I don't even like visiting lol but it's not the first time and I'm sure it won't be the last 3:06 PM

Helen: would u be up for meeting sometime this week when ur feeling a bit better? the beauty bag might cheer u up :) 3:06 PM

Peachez: Sure I don't mind that at all taken you seem real nice and all ;) 3:07 PM

Helen: :-) well that's good u can tell I'm nice :-) ok well hope ur stay in the hospital goes well and ill give u a call tomorrow about a coffee date :-) 3:59 PM

Becca

Helen: hi is this Becca?? 4:21 PM
Becca: Yes 4:22 PM
Helen: great :) how ru? 4:22 PM
Becca: I'm great, n u 4:23 PM
Helen: i'm good too :) i volunteer with a few girls, and we meet with girls on bp and give them a free beauty bag with a ton of beauty products as a free gift just to show we care. if the girl wants out or to know any other options or is in a tough spot, then we are totally there for her. if not, that's ok too and we just give u the free bag as a gift. Ru interested? :) 4:32 PM

Appendix

Becca: Unfortunately, not at this time. I really appreciate it and am glad there r ppl like u n ur organization to help those who r in need. Keep up the good work. Thanks again. 4:34 PM

Helen: aw thanks for the encouragement! it is a joy to be able to help girls who need help in any way. well save my number and if u ever change ur mind, know that we can help set you u up with job or college opportunities. a beauty bag has ur name on it any time u want one. and if ur ever in a tough spot and need immediate help we will be here. 4:38 PM

Helen: if u ever come across a girl in the life who looks like she needs help if u get me, then feel free to pass on this number too. all the best Becca, you seem like a great girl. Helen, xoxo 4:39 PM

Becca: Thank u very much and I will be sure to do that. 4:45 PM

Lisa

Helen: Hey Lisa. If u evr want out the game there r ppl in KC who can help u. Feel free 2 text me if u wana know more :) Helen (Beauty Breakthrough) 9:38 PM

Lisa: Who r u and how did u get my number? 9:41 PM

Helen: Saw ur add on back page. I volunteer for an organization that assists women to leave the life if they want and see what other options are out there 4 them :) i wana be an extra line of support. im in kansas city and here for u if you wanna know more :) Helen 9:46 PM

Lisa: I want u to get off my phone talking like ur a snitch, bitch did I call u for help ? Why are u searching thru backpage other then to turn people in? People like u should choke and die from being nosy not minding your own business 9:49 PM

Helen: ok :) we just know some girls really wanna get out but dont know how so we wanna help them if so. im here if u ever wanna talk or change ur mind :) Helen 9:50 PM

Lisa: What I do should not concern u, I'm not bothering u, I'm not hurting u, im not making u do anything, I'm not asking u for anything. How about u figure out a way for people to contact u, instead of trying to profile me. Helen ;) GO TO HELL 9:52 PM

Helen: Not wanting to offend, just want you to know that someone cares. Save my number and feel free to call if you ever need anything. 9:56 PM

Molly

Courtney: Hi Molly, if you want out of the game, there are ppl in KC who can help. Text me, Courtney
Molly: Wat u mean
Courtney: If you want to leave escorting, I saw your ad on Backpage. I can help you make it to a safe place.
Molly: I just want a real job I hate it I'm only 18 I been on my own since 12 I got college books I got to pay for that I can't afford and I refuse to give up on the one thing my so called family always told me id nvr do go to college I want my own appt n my bf in jail so I try n put money on his stuff and who are u btw like wat u do for a living
Courtney: I help people, girls, get a new start. A safe place at night, resources to help leave escorting and make it without escorting. I can help you look for a job. I'd love to do that. I'm in KC and I'd like to meet up with you for coffee and talk about options.
Molly: Id like tht but how ikur not gunna hurt? Its hard for me to just trust someone since every thing I been thru
Courtney: I understand, if you want we can talk on the phone. I can hear what sort of job you may want, and what you're studying for school. Would that be okay?
Molly: I'm going for nursing n yea u can call me
Courtney: Is now an ok time?
Molly: Yes

Ella

Helen: Hey is this Ella or Lexi...? 2:26 PM
Ella/Lexi Elf: The elves are a members only firm youll have to purchase your membership online at usacallgirl.com to be able to see an elf 2:40 PM
Helen: Ok that's helpful, ru an elf or do u just do communications? 2:41 PM
Ella/Lexi Elf: Im an elf 2:43 PM
Helen: Ok good to know :) i volunteer for beauty breakthrough, we are a nonprofit who want to give women on backpage something without wanting anything in return. We give out beauty bags full of great makeup products. Would you like one? 2:46 PM
Ella/Lexi Elf: Lol good luck darlin :-) Good to see that, although i am not in need of assistance, theres someone there to help those who are. Have a nice day. 3:03 PM

Helen: Ok :-) a lot of girls r interested in knowing more life options and we have resources and connections. Save my number if u ever change ur mind and want out of the game :-) 3:08 PM

Ella/Lexi Elf: I dont play a game sweetie and my college education gives me many options. I was attempting to be polite but you didnt take the hint and chose to use only words cheap hoes would understand. Just a helpful tip, you wont help any educated person by using offensive language. I happen to own a similar agency to yours... theres better ways to help. Again, have a nice day. 3:16 PM

Helen: I'm sorry u felt my words were offensive. As I'm sure u understand there's a whole range of levels of exploitation on backpage - we don't fully know if a girl is a 1 or a 10 on this scale but operate on the basis that whatever background - educated or not, every girl selling her body has the right to know there r options outside of an industry that frequently puts her in danger, violence, degradation and exploitation. As an educated woman i feel confident u recognize the value of such effort to reach out and let the woman know she has options, even at the risk of offense which is never intended as we only care about the women. I hope u have a great day yourself and genuinely wish u the best in all areas of your life :-) 3:26 PM

Ella/Lexi Elf: Well i assure you, i neither sell my body nor have i or anyone in my company been in danger or degraded. Just figured id let you know theres some good, Im sure it hurts to deal with the bad all the time with girls you contact... anyhow ill let you go so you can better spend your time with someone who may need it. Good luck 3:28 PM

Helen: Thank you for your best wishes, Ella. Though many of the girls I meet with are in a lot of pain and difficult circumstances, it's an absolute joy to be able to connect with them and offer assistance where possible. It's so great seeing some of the dreams for their life become reality. I hope you are living your dream and I'm encouraged to know you have not felt in danger or degraded. :) Out of interest, I googled your number before texting and it's connected to several sites where girls r advertised as escorts offering sexual services. How are you/girls in your company able to avoid clients who imagine they can buy sex?? 4:20 PM

Ella/Lexi Elf: we sell subscriptions to our porn website :-) our clients are upscale and can afford girls who demand respect. They wouldnt spend $500 on a membership plus extra time to shoot videos if they just planned to get blacklisted for being disrespectful 4:27 PM

Ariana

Helen: Hey is this Ariana's number?? 12:50 PM
Ariana: Yes 12:51 PM
Helen: Great! How are you? 12:52 PM
Ariana: I'm good and u 12:59 PM
Helen: I'm great thanks :) How long have you been doing this? The life can be tough. Have u ever wanted out? 1:02 PM
Ariana: For 6 years. Yes very badly I hate this life 1:03 PM
Helen: Wow thanks for being honest. What's keeping u in the life? What would be your dream job if u didn't have to do this? 1:43 PM
Ariana: My dream job would be to be someone who helps woman like me 1:55 PM
Helen: (Just so u know by the way I'm a girl not a guy...my name is Helen) 2:15 PM
Ariana: I'm Ashley. Nice to meet you :-D 2:15 PM
Helen: Nice to meet you too Ashley :D i love that u want to help girls! i'm actually part of a group of female volunteers called beauty breakthrough. We text girls on backpage to offer to meet up and talk through life options and bless you with a beauty bag full of free beauty products and essentials. No pressure, we would just love to connect with you! 2:21 PM
Ariana: I just feel that no woman in the world deserves to be left and forgot and raped mistreated pimped out and abused I should be dead right now from what I been through I hate this life but I'm addicted to fast money and that's what keeps me here I need help really bad or I'm sure I'm going to be in jail or dead... 2:23 PM
Helen: Yes you are right no woman ever deserves that. Ashley would u be interested to meet up to talk about where you're at and see if there's any way we can help u or connect u to ppl who can? i feel like this has come just at the right time for you 2:32 PM
Ariana: Yes I'm very interested I really want help I'm in Kansas city KS 2:34 PM
Helen: ok, we r KCMO. Are u free tomorrow afternoon at all? We cud meet in a public cafe like starbucks or something.it wud be me and another girl meeting u :)We can talk on the phone first if you'd prefer :) 3:13 PM

Appendix

Mya

Helen: Hey is this Mya?! 3:06 PM
Mya: Yes it is :) 3:13 PM
Helen: How are you doing today? 3:14 PM
Mya: I'm doing well 3:15 PM
Helen: Great to hear! Are you still in KC? 3:15 PM
Mya: Yes I am sweety 3:16 PM
Helen: Awesome! I should explain right away that I'm not a guy, I'm a girl called Helen :)
Some friends and I reach out to women in the sex industry, online and in dance clubs with gifts.
We believe all women are beautiful and awesome and so give beauty gift bags worth about $50 plus a Walmart gift card for $50 as an early Christmas gift (for you or your family) as a blessing
There's no catch, we just wanna bless you ladies this Christmas :)
If you're interested we would meet just in a local Mcdonalds near you to give you the gift.
Would you be interested in the beauty bag and gift card? 3:18 PM
Mya: Thank you so much 3:19 PM
Helen: I know this probably sounds quite random! We've done this for several years now as a way to give back as holidays can be rough sometimes. And we want the women to know there's love and support out there. 3:19 PM
Mya: Bless you 3:20 PM
Helen: Thank you! :) Is this something you'd be interested in? If so, are you available tomorrow? We can meet at a fast food spot that works for you. 3:22 PM
Mya: This sounds wonderful. I'm interested but how do I know y'all are legit. Not trying to be robbed killed raped or kidnapped 3:22 PM
Helen: Absolutely - let me just call you and explain more about who we are and answer any questions you may have. 3:23 PM
Mya: OK thank you 3:23 PM

APPENDIX B
Setting Up Google Voice

For security reasons and to maintain a sense of personal space, we recommend texting and calling from an app (e.g. Google Voice) that offers free texts and calls. Such apps can only be used through smartphones. A pseudonym email address and number are created, and you're notified of incoming calls through the app, instead of through your regular contacts. All records of texts are kept online in the pseudo email account, which helps keep record of contacts.

SETTING UP GOOGLE VOICE

1. Create a new gmail account with a pseudonym to connect Google Voice.

2. Log in to Google.com/voice.

3. Select "I want a new number."

4. Enter your cell phone number.

5. Put in confirmation code.

6. Choose a local area code.

GOOGLE VOICE PHONE SETTINGS

Under Phones:

1. Click box for "Receive text messages on this phone."

2. Click box for "Notify me of new voicemails via text."

Under Voicemail Greeting

1. You don't need to record a voicemail greeting.

2. The only box clicked should be "Transcribe voicemails" at the bottom.

3. Click the "Save changes" button.

Under Calls

1. Call Screening: On

Uncheck box "Ask unknown callers to say their name"

2. Call ID (incoming): Display my Google Voice number

(Do this because you know if it is or isn't specifically from the Google number.)

3. Caller ID (outgoing): Display my Google Voice number.

"Text Free" and "Text Plus" apps also provide a similar service to Google Voice and are worth downloading.

APPENDIX C
Sexual Integrity Commitment Form

MAKING A COMMITMENT.

Commitment #1: I commit to registering with some form of accountability software. (Note: These programs track your Internet activity and send an email to the friend of your choosing. See: www.covenanteyes.com, www.x3watch.com, or www.internetsafety.com.)

Commitment #2: I commit to not watching pornography for the purpose of illicit pleasure. (Viewing Backpage and similar sites for the purpose of outreach does not count as watching pornography.)

Commitment #3: If I stumble or relapse in the area of pornography, I will confess it immediately to an accountability partner and an intervention team leader.

Commitment #4: I commit to never do a texting outreach from online ads on my own. (This does not include follow-up texting with girls contacted during past outreaches.)

_____
Print Name

_____   _____
Sign Name   Date

APPENDIX D
Confidentiality Form

CONFIDENTIALITY

It is our desire to cultivate and maintain strong levels of trust with all exploited persons we will be working with. We want to encourage a culture of confidentiality in which we respect and honor their privacy and story, both now and in the long-term. We want to guard and protect their dignity, and we desire for them to know that they are safe when entrusting their lives and circumstances to us—bringing us into their confidence. These values should always be held as paramount; they enable us to build trust and serve these men and women with excellence and integrity.

Be wise about the personal information you share with exploited individuals. Intentionally refraining from sharing personal details about yourself with those you are reaching out to may seem extreme or even dishonest, especially when attempting to build trust. However, exploited individuals are often connected with dangerous people whose behavior can be unpredictable. The exploited individual is not the enemy, but she can be in close contact with those who seek to harm, recruit, or traffic. Because of this, it is wise to exercise caution and carefully consider what information about yourself you need to withhold—especially personal information that could be traced.

PERSONAL INFORMATION TO WITHHOLD

- Your last name
- Personal phone number (Use a Google voice number instead)
- Personal email
- (Initially at least) do not become Facebook friends
- Home address/area
- Information that could be used to trace you or family members: passport number, driver's license number, business cards (e.g. don't leave your driver's license in full view)

BE PREPARED IN ADVANCE

- Google Search your full name and email address/key words and see what comes up.

- Consider tightening security on:

    - Websites

    - Blogs

    - Social Media

Explore additional security measures with Facebook. Look under privacy settings and make sure your profile is only viewable to friends. Don't display any photos of your house or a close family member's house. Remove location tags on your profile/history, including Google maps of your/a friend's house.

Important to remember: We never want to lie. We are seeking to build a culture of trust, and that is based on truth. But we can refrain and use caution with what we do share.

CONFIDENTIALITY ON OUR PART TOWARDS THE EXPLOITED INDIVIDUALS

All individuals we work with reserve the right to the following:

- Confidentiality

- To be treated with dignity and respect

- Respect of privacy

- Self-determination in identifying and setting goals and plans

- To be treated with cultural sensitivity

- To receive services based on full and informed consent

- To be clearly informed in a language understood by the individual regarding the purpose of the services offered and administered

- Reasonable access to personal records

- We give all exploited individuals we work with a pseudonym (code name). To protect their identity, we refer to them by this pseudonym to all persons with the exception of:

  - The individual

  - Our tri-team (members B and C)

  - Any individuals involved directly in their security

  - Law enforcement or medical professionals

- All team members should keep a record of all information regarding contact with the exploited individuals through meeting forms (see Appendix F). This information is to be kept confidential.

- All personal and sensitive details of the various circumstances of the exploited individuals and their identities should remain exclusively within the team.

- Details of our outreach and contact with the individuals must not ever be referenced or mentioned on Facebook (statuses, wall posts) or other public social media. We do this out of our commitment to respect the individual and honor their confidentiality.

- The vision for the intervention team community is that we are united as a body and give support, prayer, and encouragement to one another as we seek to reach out to those being exploited. It is vital that we do not process heavy situations alone or feel we must isolate ourselves to maintain confidentiality. We will need to lean on one another, and our weekly team meetings provide an opportunity to share things we are dealing with and receive prayer, encouragement, and empathetic understanding.

Important Additional Information Regarding Confidentiality

- If you discover that an exploited individual you are working with is abusing or neglecting a child, you must inform social services, even at the risk of breaking trust. In these cases, the care and safety of the child must be the priority. See www.childhelp.org or call the Childhelp National Child Abuse Hotline 1-800-4-A-CHILD (1-800-422-4453).

- If an individual you are working with vocalizes that they are having suicidal thoughts, you should go on to establish the following with them: Possible past actions, present threats, whether or not they are alone, their location and phone number, and whether or not they have dependent children living with them. Make clear notes of the conversation and actions taken. Consider calling the National Suicide Prevention Lifeline at 1-800-273-TALK (8255) or in an emergency call 911.

APPENDIX E
Reporting Forms

If you make contact with an individual from Backpage, there needs to be documentation of the process. We highly recommended that you keep an accurate file on each individual you are meeting with. This helps you keep track of their story and allows you to determine the best ways to support them. Also, include valuable information about expenses, resources you provided, their dreams for life, and tri-team information. The team leader will not be attending every meeting the tri-team goes on, so it is extremely helpful for the leader to have a record of the meetings taking place and the details surrounding each one.

I. Save this information in the exploited individual's file.

- First text conversation that leads to a meeting into a Word document (paste from Google voice online history).

- A copy of one of the individual's Backpage ads. You can copy and paste this into a Word doc and crop out any nudity.

- The History form (see Appendix G) must be filled out by one tri-team member who attended the first meeting. Please complete it using the information you learned about the individual during the meeting and send it to the team leader on that same day.

- After every subsequent meeting, the Meeting form (see Appendix F) must be filled out by only one tri-team member and sent to the team leader on that same day.

- Meeting forms can be filled out by hand during the post-meeting debrief or in a Word document and sent via email.

- After you have been in relationship with an individual for several months, it may not be necessary to fill out a Meeting form each time, but speak to the team leader first.

APPENDIX F
Meeting Forms

Complete after every in-person contact with the individuals you are serving.

Your name	Tri-Team Members	
Location of meeting		Date
Where did you meet the individual? ☐ At public location ☐ At their home	Where?	Address
Real name of individual	Pseudonym	
Did you meet for? ☐ Breakfast ☐ Lunch ☐ Dinner ☐ Coffee ☐ Other _____		Did you pay for the individual's food/drink? (Y/N)	Cost
Relationship Status		Transgendered (Y/N)	
List any additional places you went:	List any additional items you bought:		
Was there a security detail? (Y/N)	Who?		
How long did security detail follow? (circle one) ☐ Pick-up ☐ Drive to ☐ Drop-off ☐ Partial ☐ Entire meeting ☐ Other _____			
Please describe the individual's emotional state throughout the meeting:			

Form continued on next page

Intervention Manual

Please list services that you provided to the individual: (prayer, purchased items, social services, etc.)

Please describe any new stories or history that were brought up:

Please list your recommendations for the next steps to take to assist individual:

How you are feeling in your heart since the meeting?

Additional notes:

APPENDIX G
History Form

Complete after the first contact with the individual you are serving.

Your name	Tri-Team Members	

How did contact occur?

Real name of individual	Pseudonym	Address
Phone Number	Hometown	

Hair Color	Eye Color	Height	Weight	Age	Gender

Relationship Status		Transgendered (Y/N)
Length of time in your area	Means of transportation	Driver's license

Additional Notes

Is the individual making income through prostitution?

Are any other individuals living off the proceeds off of his/her prostitution?	If so, who?

Sources of income other than prostitution: (disability, food stamps, Medicaid)

City where primary exploitation occurred:	Age when exploitation occurred:
List any other cities where exploitation occurred:	Length of time exploited:

Form continued on next page

Intervention Manual

Did trafficking occur as defined by force, fraud or coercion or underage sale of sex involved?:				
Was the individual involved in any of the following?: (check all that apply) ☐ Prostitution ☐ Strip Clubs ☐ Massage ☐ Parlor Service ☐ Pornography ☐ Phone Sex ☐ Escort ☐ Sex for drugs, money, or survival needs				

Is there any history of? ☐ Foster Care ☐ Alcohol ☐ Juvenile Parental ☐ Drugs Runaway ☐ Homelessness ☐ Divorce ☐ Prison Rehab ☐ Incest ☐ Mental Illness	Who does the individual currently live with? ☐ Pimp ☐ Friend ☐ Family ☐ Streets ☐ Boyfriend ☐ Shelter ☐ Alone ☐ Other

Does the individual have children? (Y/N)	If so, how many?	Ages?	Do the children live with the individual? (Y/N)
If female, is she pregnant?	If so, due date?	List any history of abuse ☐ Sexual ☐ Spiritual ☐ Verbal ☐ Satanic ritual abuse ☐ Physical ☐ Other ☐ Emotional	
List any religious affiliations			

History of mental illness	Is she currently on medication? (Y/N)	If so, for what?
List any other medical conditions		

Has there been a history of attempted suicide? (Y/N)	If so, how many times?	Currently suicidal?
Is there any history of abortion? (Y/N)		

Any additional addresses associated with the individual?	Additional notes?

Form continued on next page

Appendix

Please give a detailed description of the individual's introduction to sexual exploitation (if known):

Please give a detailed entry about the individual's history of exploitation (if known):

Please describe the individual's goals and/or dreams (if known):

Please list any positive support or relationships that are currently in the individual's life:

Please describe any current predatory or abusive relationships the individual is in:

Please describe the individual's family situation (if known):

APPENDIX I
Palermo Protocols

United Nations-Protocol to Prevent, Suppress, and Punish Trafficking in Persons Especially Women and Children, supplementing the United Nations Convention against Transnational Organized Crime (Palermo Protocols)

- "Trafficking in persons" shall mean the recruitment, transportation, transfer, harboring or receipt of persons, by means of the threat or use of force or other forms of coercion, of abduction, of fraud, of deception, of the abuse of power or of a position of vulnerability or of the giving or receiving of payments or benefits to achieve the consent of a person having control over another person, for the purpose of exploitation. Exploitation shall include, at a minimum, the exploitation of the prostitution of others or other forms of sexual exploitation, forced labor or services, slavery or practices similar to slavery, servitude or the removal of organs.

i. The consent of a victim of trafficking in persons to the intended exploitation set forth in subparagraph (a) of this article shall be irrelevant where any of the means set forth in subparagraph (a) have been used;

ii. The recruitment, transportation, transfer, harboring, or receipt of a child for the purpose of exploitation shall be considered "trafficking in persons" even if this does not involve any of the means set forth in subparagraph (a) of this article;

iii. "Child" shall mean any person under 18 years of age.

Made in the USA
Middletown, DE
20 December 2021